Brig.-General S. C. E. HERRING, C.M.G., D.S.O.
C. de G. (French), Croix D'Officer (French), Legion of Honour (French).

THE CHRONICLE OF THE

45th BATTALION A.I.F.

by

Major J.E. Lee

D.S.O., M.C.

" Stand still ————
Let me review the scene,
And summon from the shadowy Past
The forms that once have been" ————
Longfellow

The Naval & Military Press Ltd

in association with

The Imperial War Museum
Department of Printed Books

Published jointly by
The Naval & Military Press Ltd
Unit 10 Ridgewood Industrial Park,
Uckfield, East Sussex,
TN22 5QE England
Tel: +44 (0) 1825 749494
Fax: +44 (0) 1825 765701
www.naval-military-press.com
www.military-genealogy.com
www.militarymaproom.com

and

The Imperial War Museum, London
Department of Printed Books
www.iwm.org.uk

Printed and bound in Great Britain by
CPI Antony Rowe, Chippenham and Eastbourne

THE CHRONICLE

OF

THE 45th BATTALION, A.I.F.

BY

MAJOR J. E. LEE, D.S.O., M.C.

CONTENTS.

APPENDICES.

PHOTOGRAPHS.

Brig.-General S. C. E. Herring, C.M.G., D.S.O., C. de G. (French), Croix D'Officer (French), Legion of Honour (French)

Major J. E. Lee, D.S.O., M.C.

Lt.-Col. S. L. Perry, D.S.O., M.C.

Lt.-Col. A. S. Allen, D.S.O., C. de G. (France)

Lt.-Col. N. M. Loutit, D.S.O. and Bar

MAPS.

Northern Egypt
The Area of Fighting in Flanders
The Somme Area
Northern France

FOREWORD

BY

General W. R. Birdwood, G.C.M.G., K.C.B. Indian Army, formerly G.O.C. A.I.F.

I have been asked to write a foreword for the regimental history of 45th Battalion of the A.I.F. While very glad to be able to do this, I fear I approach the subject with hesitation, realising how unlikely I am to do anything like justice to it. I say this, as the events now chronicled seem to belong almost to bygone history, and after so many years since the conclusion of the Armistice, it becomes almost impossible to carry one's mind back to the doings of individuals—or even always to individual battalions, who made history and did such glorious work throughout the War. Also the request to write this foreword has come to me, in what one might almost call one of the far distant corners of the world, as I happen at the present moment to be inspecting one of the outposts of our Empire at the extreme end of the North West Frontier of India—viz., Chitral. Here I am without notes of reference of any sort, but the rugged and mountainous country brings one's memory back to some of the more difficult and precipitous portions of the Gallipoli Peninsula. With such memories for all of us who were there, must always be associated the 25th April 1915, when Australia leapt into manhood—or rather I should say into nationhood by the valour of her sons.

On the 25th April, 1915, there was no 45th battalion in the A.I.F., but no records of the 45th could be complete without mention of their parent—the 13th battalion of the A.I.F. Well do I remember the arrival of this battalion with the 4th Brigade in Egypt in January, 1915, and well do I remember the magnificent work performed by it throughout the whole of our time on the Peninsula during 1915. This battalion was raised in New South Wales—the 5th complete battalion to leave that State, and well did it hold its own with the 1st, 2nd, 3rd and 4th battalions from New South Wales.

On our return from the Peninsula in December, 1915, and before we proceeded to France it was found essential to increase the Australian Forces to complete up to a strength of five divisions—a force quite unthought of—and probably considered impossible when the first division left Australia in 1914. I realised that the only way in which it would be possible to organise new units rapidly and efficiently would be to break up our old force, utilising its traditions, training, officers, non-commissioned officers and men to form new divisions. I need hardly say how unpopular such a method naturally must be to already formed units, in which officers and men had been fighting side by side throughout all those weary months at Gallipoli, and during which every individual was fully satisfied that his particular battalion was the best, not only in the A.I.F. but in the British Empire or even in the world. Realising this as I did, it was naturally a matter of the greatest regret that I came to the conclusion that in the interests of our Empire such breaking up was essential, and we consequently divided all our first 16 battalions into half, and completed the whole 32 battalions thus formed by reinforcements and recruits, who were waiting for us in Egypt. On these re-organisations the 45th sprang from the loins of the 13th. I know well when I assured all concerned that it would not be long before the newly-formed units took their places alongside of the old stocks, that they would more than justify their existence and would prove themselves every bit as good as their parents—that I was not believed. It is quite unnecessary for me now to say how completely my statement was justified, and the 45th from its formation at Tel-el-Kebir in March, 1916, until the conclusion of the War, proved to the world what can be done by unflinching bravery—determination to win through, and good leadership.

It is only necessary to mention the names of Pozieres, Messines, Bullecourt and Passchendaele, to realise some of the hard fighting in which the battalion was engaged and during which it lost 36 officers and 654 other ranks.

This regimental history will give details of its fighting and of the honours gained, so it is unnecessary for me (even if it were possible) to go into these. I am only glad to be able to testify now to the bravery and great spirit shown by all ranks throughout the War, and to express my gratitude and affection to those who proved themselves the best of friends and most loyal of comrades throughout the years it was my privilege to be in command of the Australian Forces.

I sincerely trust that happiness and prosperity may be the lot of the survivors, and to one and all of the 45th battalion who may be reading this chronicle, I send my greetings, remembrances and grateful thanks for past work done.

W. R. BIRDWOOD, General,

Chitral, June 1924.   Australian Military Forces.

FOREWORD

BY

Brig. General S. C. E. Herring, C.M.G., D.S.O.

The 45th Bn. was formed in Egypt shortly after the Evacuation and, as a backbone, it started with two companies and half the officers of the gallant old Thirteenth. To build up, equip, and train a Battalion to take its part in the great war was no light task, but the 45th Bn. had the great advantage of having 300 officers and men who had been on active service at Gallipoli, many of them veterans of the whole campaign there. So the task of selecting officers and N.C.O.'s was not as difficult as it would have been if there had only been untried troops to pick from. When the Bn. left for France the whole of the Bn. staff, the four Company Commanders, half the Company Officers and a large majority of the senior N.C.O.'s were all men who had seen service in Gallipoli.

As a C.O. I always placed loyalty to the Battalion, and incidentally to the senior officers, as one of the most essential things. If Units pull together as one, the general result is always first-class, and, at times the almost impossible is achieved. This loyalty was always given as a matter of course as far as the 45th Bn. was concerned, and in my opinion was a great factor towards the success achieved.

From the word go, the 45th was a happy family and the esprit de corps was very strong. They looked to their C.O. and Senior Officers for leadership and no matter what the task was, the Officers and Men as one set to work to carry out the job in the most prompt and efficient manner.

The Bn. established its name as a first-class fighting unit at Pozieres, the first big action it took part in. Pozieres was a trying christening for any force, as it entailed the defence of an exposed ridge recently captured from the Germans and one which they, the Germans, were particularly anxious to retake. For the first 48 hours the Bn. together with the remainder of the 12th Brigade was subjected to an almost continuous shelling by the enemy, and the whole period in the line was like a nightmare to all members of the Bn.

The losses sustained by the Bn. during this action were of necessity severe, but it established a name for steadiness and coolness in action and set up a standard that it never lowered throughout the remainder of the War. The Divisional Commander when addressing the Brigade after Pozieres, after remarking on the heavy continuous shelling the Brigade had been under, finished his address with these words: "You have many stiff battles ahead of you, but in my opinion never again will you be subjected to such heavy and continuous shell fire."

The hardest actions fought by the Bn. were Pozieres, Messines, and Dernacourt, and in the two latter, as in the former, the Bn. came out of the fighting with flying colors. The Bn.'s fighting record generally was a brilliant one, as this history together with the Battle Honours awarded, will testify. Naturally I am very proud of its record, and if I were asked what in my opinion were the outstanding features of its career I think I would reply: "They never gave up a position once taken. They never failed to respond to the call of an additional effort, and their losses, compared with the work done, were always comparatively moderate."

I do not propose to discuss in this short foreword the merits of any particular Officers or Men. We had so many sterling soldiers in the Bn. that it would be unfair to pick out individuals, but there is one fact I would specially like to mention and that is that over 75 per cent. of the Officers of the Bn. were N.C.O.'s and men who had been promoted in the field on account of special leadership and bravery in action. As a type of the class of Officer that helped to make the 45th what it was I would like to mention: Major Howden, M.C. and Bar. In August, 1915, Howden was a bombing Corporal in the 13th Bn. and in February, 1917, a Major in the 45th Bn., and but for his untimely death he would have commanded a Bn. a few months later; a brave and gallant soldier whose death was mourned not only by the whole Bn. but the whole Division.

In conclusion I wish, on behalf of the Committee, to thank Major J. E. Lee, D.S.O., M.C., for so ably writing the history of the Bn.

When selecting a Bn. staff one of the most difficult positions to fill is that of Adjutant, the qualifications required are very exacting, he must be capable and efficient, and it is also essential that he be tactful. Lee had all these qualifications, and,

Major J. E. LEE. D.S.O., M.C.

in addition, he had proved himself a particularly gallant officer. (Lee was a Duntroon Graduate, an original 13th Bn. Officer, and had seen a lot of fighting at Gallipoli). Therefore, when a few days after the formation of the 45th, Major (then Lieut.) Lee reported back to the 13th Bn. from hospital (he had been severely wounded in Gallipoli in August, 1915). I made up my mind that I must secure him as Adjutant of the 45th Bn.

Major Lee's service to the Bn. proved invaluable, first as an Adjutant during that trying time of training and equipping the Bn., the march to the Canal and the outpost work there, and during the move to France and the heavy fighting of Pozieres. At Pozieres he was appointed Second-in-Command, and did sterling work during the fighting in that terrible winter 1916/7. In 1917 he left to join the staff of the 12th Brigade, much to the regret of the whole Bn.

Major Lee was always jealous of the honour of the 45th Bn. Nothing but the best would suit him whether fighting or training. An Officer with high ideals, and the ability and pluck to carry on anything that he thought was in the best interests of the Bn.

SYDNEY C. E. HERRING.

CHAPTER I.

THE FORMATION OF THE BATTALION.

After the evacuation from Gallipoli at the end of December, 1915, the Australian Imperial Force had returned to Egypt to be re-organised and equipped for future operations.   Many thousands of reinforcements from Australia had arrived and were still reaching Egypt and it was decided that Austraalia could maintain five divisions.   The 1st and 2nd Divisions were already formed; the 3rd Division was to be organised in Australia and the 4th and 5th Divisions were to be formed in Egypt from units already in existence and from those to be formed.   The 4th Division was to consist of the 4th, 12th and 13th Infantry Brigades.   The 4th Infantry Brigade had been in existence since November, 1914, and, as part of the New Zealand and Australian Division, had been at the Landing at Anzac and had served with marked distinction during the whole of the Gallipoli campaign. Its units were the 13th Bn. from N.S.W., the 14th Bn. from Victoria, the 15th Bn. from Queensland and Tasmania, and the 16th Bn. from W.A. and S.A.

The 12th Infantry Brigade was formed from the 4th Infantry Brigade in the following manner:—Two companies were transferred from each of the battalions in the latter brigade to form the nucleus of each of the battalions in the new brigade. Thus the 45th Bn. was formed from the 13th, the 46th from the 14th, the 47th from the 15th and the 48th from the 16th.   The 13th Infantry Brigade was formed in a somewhat similar manner from the 3rd Infantry Brigade of the 1st Division.

After the 13th Battalion returned to Egypt from Gallipoli, it proceeded to Moascar; but in February, 1916, it was camped in the desert at Tel-el-Kebir, on the railway line between Cairo and Ismailiya.   About the middle of February orders were received for the formation of the 45th Bn. from the 13th. Naturally the great majority of the officers and other ranks did not want to leave their old battalion which had established such a fine record on the Peninsula.   In order to give the new unit a good start, it was decided that, with the exception of the officers and warrant officers, two complete companies should be transferred to form the nucleus of the 45th.   Its commanding officer was to be Major S. C. E. Herring, then second-in-command of the 13th Bn., which he had commanded with distinction on

Gallipoli. The C.O. 13th Bn. and Major Herring chose alternately their officers, the company commanders and specialist officers of the 13th Bn., however, remaining with that unit. Major Herring also had the option of selecting any warrant office or non-commissioned officer whom he intended to promote to commissioned or warrant rank.

On March 2nd, 1916, the two companies of the 13th Bn. to be transferred (i.e., "B" and "D" Companies), paraded with the officers, warrant and non-commissioned officers who had been selected for the 45th. These troops, after they had been inspected by the Brig.-General Glasfurd, the Commander of the 12th Infantry Brigade, were formally handed over by the C.O. 13th to the C.O. 45th. It seemed then, a very sad day for these officers, n.c.o.'s and men who had helped to make the name of the 13th Bn., to be transferred compulsorily from their old regiment. Anyone who has been a soldier realises what a tremendous moral force esprit-de-corps is. But these men, who had already proved themselves soldiers, went to their new unit determined to make the 45th Bn. a worthy sister to the 13th.

On the completion of the formal transfer, the 45th Bn. marched off to its new camp, which had been partially prepared. "B" Company was then split up and formed "A" and "B" Companies and from "D" Company were formed "C" and "D." On the first day of its existence, the battalion's strength was 12 officers and 361 other ranks. With the exception of one, all the officers had seen active service on Gallipoli, 4 had been officers in the original 13th when it left Australia in 1914, 7 had been promoted from the ranks on Gallipoli, and the other one was a reinforcement officer. Of the 361 other ranks, 278 had been on Gallipoli, and the remainder were from the 9th and 10th Reinforcements which had joined the 13th Bn. at Moascar. Amongst the men with service were the machine gunners, signallers and pioneers.

Another indication of the generous treatment by the 13th Bn. was the donation of half its regimental fund to the 45th. This goodwill had a lasting effect during the remainder of the war, and there was always a very strong bond of sympathy between the two battalions, which was fostered by the two regimental Comforts Funds Committees working together in Sydney.

The 45th Bn. was fortunate in having Lt.-Colonel Herring as its first commanding officer. Not only had he been with the 13th from its inception but he had a good eye for picking his men, and he chose with discrimination the officers and the n.c.o.'s who were to receive commissions. He also made a careful selection of those who were to be warrant officers and sergeants, some of whom he selected at the Base. It was to the wise selection at the outset of the officers, warrant and non-commissioned officers that much of the battalion's success later was due.

A busy time followed in organising the sections, platoons and companies. A practical system of interior economy was inaugurated, special attention being paid to sanitation, hygiene and the cooking arrangements. Those who were at Tel-el-Kebir will remember how the Brigadier kept his battalions up to the mark. General Glasfurd, a very fine type of the British regular officer, was in Australia on exchange duty as Director of Military Training when war broke out, and had left Australia with the 1st Division on the General Staff. On March 10th, the battalion was inspected by Major-General Cox, the Divisional Commander, who was an Indian Army officer of great ability and experience and who had commanded the Indian Brigade, including. the Ghurkas, on Gallipoli.

It was essential that the battalion should be fully equipped and, as the men had only their personal requirements, the Quartermaster, Lieut. Rankin, and R.Q.M.S. Neaves had a busy time in obtaining from a much harassed Ordnance Service all the mobilisation equipment. As there were so many newly-formed battalions, the early and successful equipping of the 45th depended largely on the ingenuity and persistence of the Q.M. and his Staff. Until it received its regimental transport, use was made of that of the 13th Bn. for the conveyance of stores and rations.

The training of the unit was now commenced. A fair proportion of the men were of course trained soldiers but, owing to the peculiar nature of the warfare on Gallipoli, much "refresher-training" was necessary. Of those who had not been on the Peninsula, the majority had completed their company training, but half had been without rifles since their arrival in Egypt. Unfortunately there were no facilities for the carrying out of musketry practices at Tel-el-Kebir. The individual training of young officers and n.c.o.'s was proceeded with by the holding of special company and battalion classes for them.

At this time the strength of the unit was constantly fluctuating owing to the arrival of reinforcements and to the transferring of large numbers to the newly-created divisional units, e.g., artillery brigades, pioneer battalion, and machine gun companies. On March 16th, the 45th received a big batch of reinforcements numbering 5 officers and 459 other ranks. These men belonged to the 14th Reinforcements of the 1st Bn., the

2nd of the 30th Bn., and 10th, 11th and 12th Reinforcements of the 13th Bn. (all N.S.W. units). These arrivals and departures hindered the organising and training of the battalion, which was also rendered difficult by the inoculation of the troops against para typhoid, and the supplying of numerous working parties for the construction of necessary camp buildings. By this time the officers' mess was organised as well as one for the sergeants.

On March 22nd H.R.H. the Prince of Wales, accompanied by General Birdwood, rode through the camp lines after seeing the men at their training. His youthful appearance and sense of duty appealed to the men.

The appointment of second-in-command of the battalion was filled by Major W. J. Rowland from the 53rd Bn. and Major D. K. Chapman from the 49th Bn. became the senior company commander. These two appointments were made because the company commanders were young, their average age being about 23 years. Captain C. B. Hopkins, a Duntroon graduate, who was very popular with all ranks, was transferred to the 14th Infantry Brigade as Staff Captain, and was killed later at the tragic battle of Fromelles in July, 1916. The appointment of Adjutant had been filled early in March by Captain J. E. Lee, M.C. 13th Bn., a graduate of Duntroon. The strength of the officers was increased by the conferring of commissions upon 8 n.c.o.'s, of whom 5 had seen service on Gallipoli.

With plenty of work the time at Tel-el-Kebir passed quickly. The surrounding country was certainly uninteresting except for the wonderful sweet water canal and the historic battlefield of Tel-el-Kebir, on which traces of the Egyptian trenches where Arabi Pasha in 1882 was so completely defeated by the British, were still visible. Towards the end of March preparations were set afoot for the first of the many moves that the battalion was to make. This was a march to the Suez Canal where the division was to relieve the 1st Division, already on its way to France.

CHAPTER II.

THE MARCH FROM TEL-EL-KEBIR TO SERAPEUM.

This march to Serapeum was carried out by the brigades of the 4th and 5th Divisions. The 12th Infantry Brigade commenced its trek across the desert on March 26th. The dress was marching order with 120 rounds, of S.A.A. per man and full water bottles; khaki drill jackets, helmets and breeches with puttees. Marching order meant that in addition to the rifle, bayonet, ammunition, web equipment and entrenching tool, the soldier also carried a great-coat, personal effects, and a haversack containing mess tin and unexpended portion of the day's ration. In all, he carried on his person a dead weight of 61 pounds, no light load for a march over desert sands.

For this march, the battalion was allotted two limbered G.S. Wagons and 50 camels, for the transport of blankets, rations, cooking utensils and officers' baggage. The remainder of the stores, including the men's kitbags were sent by train. It was realised that its success depended largely on the preliminary arrangements which included the preparation of the men's boots and socks, instructions regarding the drinking of water and the care of feet, and the correct loading of camels. The camels were in charge of native drivers from the Indian Camel Corps and Pte. G. Parke acted as interpreter. Lieut. Holman, the Machine Gun Officer, was in charge of the battalion's camel train.

At 4 p.m. on March 27th the battalion, some 21 officers and 534 other ranks strong started on this memorable march. Many other battalions were already on the move, and this twentieth century "Exodus" was a remarkable sight with thousands of men and hundreds of camels all moving to the east. For the first day the marching was good as the ground was hard. The route lay along the north bank of the sweet water canal and late that evening the battalion, after having marched 12 miles, bivouacked for the night west of Mahsama.

General Glasfurd, who had had considerable experience in African campaigns, had wisely ordered that the marching had to be done in the comparative coolness of the mornings and evenings and that during the heat of the day the troops should rest. In supervising the march of his brigade he was ably assisted by Major J. Peck, the Brigade Major, and Captain W. Inglis, the Staff Captain.

At 6 the next morning the battalion marched to Mahsama where a good breakfast, prepared under difficulties owing to the scarcity of water, by Q.M.'s staff and cooks, awaited the troops. This halting place was close to the sweet water canal, the water of which the men were warned against drinking or bathing in, owing to the prevalence of the bilharzia disease in Egypt. After resting until 3.30 p.m. the battalion marched again, with the camels carrying the blankets, etc., in rear, but the remainder of the transport crossed the railway and followed the canal to Moascar. The march across loose desert sand continued until 8.30 p.m. when the battalion bivouacked at Maghana. The men who had not yet been hardened by long route marches began to show signs of weariness. Many of them were recently back from hospital, where they had been suffering from wounds or sickness, whilst others were recent reinforcements. Their feet began to chafe and blister, and added to this, were the physical discomforts caused by the heat of the sun, desert winds, loose sands and limited supply of water.

Early in the morning of March 29th, the battalion began to trek again. Unfortunately, owing to the lack of water breakfast could not be obtained until Moascar was reached. This stage of five miles between Maghana and Moascar was the worst one of the whole march. As the majority of the men had drunk the water in their bottles, a hurried collection was made of the empty bottles which were packed off on the fastest camels to be filled at Moascar. The full bottles were brought back post haste to the battalion which was plodding along through the heavy sand. Very few of the men fell out, and at 8.30 a.m. Moascar was reached, where the battalion was provided with a breakfast and rested for the remainder of the day, being very hospitably received by the New Zealanders, many of whom were old friends of Gallipoli days. Despite this very trying march, many of the men had sufficient energy to walk across to Lake Ismailia for a swim.

At 6 a.m. next day, the battalion marched out from Moascar. A small number of men whose feet were in a bad condition from marching were carried by the Field Ambulance by the order of the R.M.O., Captain Elwell. The route to Serapeum lay along a narrow road on the bank of the sweet water canal. This roadway was congested with the transport of other units, and the mixing of camel trains caused considerable argument amongst the harassed drivers. One of the four riding horses that the battalion possessed at the time, demonstrated its natural dislike to the camels by jumping into the canal, and became so badly staked that it had to be shot.

As the battalion began to arrive at Serapeum, the sand became very loose and a sand storm arose. Eventually the Suez Canal was reached and the 45th crossed at Serapeum by a pontoon bridge and marched to a tented camp about a mile east of the canal. On arrival at Serapeum it was met by the Advance Party under Captain Allen and welcomed by the 13th, which immediately provided a meal for all ranks. With the exception of 15 men who were carried by the Field Ambulance, the whole battalion finished the march which was a fine achievement and showed that the march discipline was already of a high standard. Those who took part in it will never forget that difficult march across the desert from Tel-el-Kebir to Serapeum.

CHAPTER III.

EAST OF THE SUEZ CANAL.

At Serapeum the battalion was on the western fringe of the Sinai desert. Several days were spent in resting after the recent march and, as the Suez Canal was in close proximity, full advantages were taken of the opportunities to bathe. Here the battalion took on its strength 160 men from the 1st Infantry Brigade and a draft of 90 reinforcements from the 1st and 8th Training Battalions. All these men had to be fitted out with equipment although the battalion was still deficient in many of its mobilisation stores.

On April 3rd, the battalion marched to railhead, which was the terminus of a light railway running six miles into the desert. The next day it relieved the 9th and 10th Light Horse Regiments in the defences on a front of 12 miles. All four companies were in the line and Battalion Headquarters were three miles east of railhead. Rations and water were sent out direct to the companies by camel transport, for which the latter supplied guides. For drinking and washing purposes, each man was limited to one gallon of water per diem, not much for men living in the desert in summer-time. This water was brought in trucks to railhead and then carried in metal containers or "fantassies" on camels out to the battalion. The drivers of the camels were Egyptians who had to be very carefully supervised during the loading as, having each two or more camels to look after, they

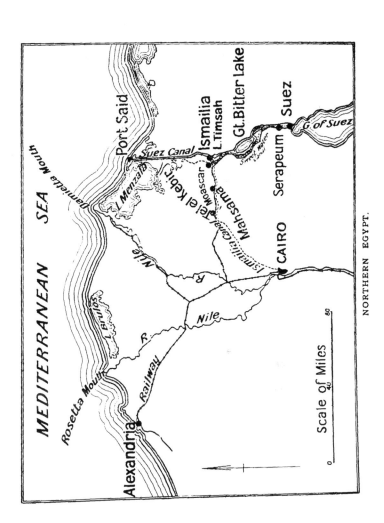

NORTHERN EGYPT.

were liable to start off without their full load of precious water or rations.

The posts occupied by the platoons were usually about a mile apart, and were so sited that they were difficult to locate at close range even in daylight. As a small Turkish force was about 50 miles distant in an oasis, and in the desert were Bedouins, the trenches had to be manned at night, but, during the day, observation groups were sufficient. New trenches were dug and revetted, the old ones kept clear of the drifting sand, and wire entanglements erected. The surrounding sand hills made a scene of absolute desolation; not a bush nor blade of grass, nor any sign of animal or bird life was to be seen, but flies and insects were a plague.

Lieut.-Colonel Herring departed on five weeks leave to England on April 10th and Major Rowland temporarily assumed command. The next day the battalion was relieved by the 47th and moved back to the camp at railhead. Here training was resumed, special attention being paid to that of signallers, bombers and Lewis gunners. A Lewis gun section, under Lieut. J. Holman, had taken the place of the Vickers machine gun section which had been incorporated in the Brigade Machine Gun Company. A course of musketry and intensive training was carried out and the officers were put through a riding course. Despite the hot weather, all this was cheerfully done, as it was common knowledge that the division was to go to France as soon as it was equipped and trained.

The weather was now becoming rapidly worse as the "khamsin" had commenced to blow. During this unpleasant weather, the battalion was frequently marched to the Canal which was 5 miles away, for a swim. On April 25th the 4th Division celebrated Anzac Day by holding aquatic sports on the Canal. The 45th was the champion battalion in the Division chiefly due to Lieut. Cornish winning most of the principal swimming events. At these sports, H.R.H. the Prince of Wales and General Godley, who commanded the Second Anzac Corps in which the 4th Division was incorporated, were present. Three days later the battalion took part in divisional manoeuvres, in which the leading platoons and companies showed that the training was proceeding on sound lines.

Owing to the Turks becoming more active in the Sinai Peninsula, it was decided that the defences should be more strongly held, and on May 5th the battalion took over a sector of the front 3 miles in extent. As the General Staff anticipated a Turkish offensive, more wire entanglements were erected and at dawn the whole battalion stood to arms.   Gradually all hope of an attack faded away and on May 11th the 45th was relieved by the 50th Bn., and a week later moved back to Serapeum. This life in the desert was for a short time good training for the troops, and they were looking very fit.

The strength of the battalion had been increased at the end of April by the arrival of 220 men belonging to the 13th, 14th and 15th Reinforcements of the 13th Bn. and to the 1st Training Battalion.   The final stage in equipping the unit for service on the western front was now begun.   Whilst at Serapeum the battalion took part in divisional night operations to test the inner defences of the Canal.   About this time, Captain E. L. Salier, M.C., of the Northumberland Fusiliers, a Tasmanian who had joined the Regular Army in pre-war days, was appointed Brigade Major.

The senior officers of the battalion, who, when in the 13th Bn., had learnt the great value of a brass band to a unit decided to form one in the 45th.   They called for voluntary subscriptions from all ranks, and in one week obtained sufficient money to purchase the instruments.   These were bought in London by the C.O., who returned on May 28th, and were sent to Port Said where Lt. Drinkwater received them and took them to France whither the battalion was about to go.

On June 1st the 45th at full war establishment and complete in equipment, entrained at Serapeum, and next day arrived at Alexandria where it embarked in the "Kinfauns Castle," with the exception of the regimental transport, which was in the "Kingstonian."   The battalion had been in existence only three months, but its esprit-de-corps was already so strong that it was keen to fight as a unit.   Every one was glad to be out of Egypt, and was looking forward expectantly to the life in France. Yet although it had many disadvantages, Egypt was a good training ground for troops and those who had not been on Gallipoli learnt to endure hardships of which they had had no experience in Australia.   More important still was the fact that these men, who for two months had been guarding the Suez Canal, realised how vital is the safety of that waterway to the British Empire.

When the battalion left for France in June, 1916, the officers and warrant-officers were as follows:—

Battalion Headquarters.

Commanding Officer.	Lieut.-Colonel S. C. E. Herring.
Second in Command.	Major W. J. Rowland.
Adjutant.	Captain J. E. Lee, M.C.
Medical Officer.	Captain L. B. Elwell.
Quarter Master.	Lieut. B. E. Rankin.
Transport Officer	Lieut. W. N. Tingcombe.
Chaplain	Captain Ingamells. ,
Regimental Sergeant Major.	R. S. M. E. V. Tuson, M.M.
Regimental Quarter Master Sergeant.	R.Q.M.S. H. H . Neaves.

"A" Company.

Company Commander.	Captain S. L. Perry.
Second-in-Command.	Captain A. S. Allen.
Platoon Commanders.	Lieutenants Cornish, Drinkwater, P. V. Murray and Ferguson.
Company Sergeant Major.	C.S.M. J. Young.
Company Quarter Master Sergeant.	C.Q.M.S. T. McKinley.

"B" Company.

Company Commander.	Captain G. E. Knox.
Platoon Commanders.	Lieuts. Abel, Schadel, Hand, Russell and H. B. Allen.
Company Sergeant Major.	C.S.M. Bradford.
Company Quarter Master Sergeant.	C.Q.M.S. J. H. Sorrell, M.M.

"C" Company.

Company Commander.	Captain H. C. Howden.
Platoon Commanders.	Lieuts. L. Young, Varley, Garling, Boyd and Meggitt.
Company Sergeant Major.	C.S.M. Bailey.
Company Quarter Master Sergeant.	C.Q.M.S. Marriott.

"D" Company.

Company Commander.	Major D. K. Chapman.
Second-in-Command.	Captain R. T. Tarrant.
Platoon Commanders.	Lieuts. Kirdwood, E. Davies, Draper and McLean.
Company Sergeant Major.	C.S.M. Crooks.
Company Quarter Master Sergeant.	C.Q.M.S. Dietze.

CHAPTER IV.

THE ARRIVAL IN FRANCE.

The "Kinfauns Castle" with the 45th Battalion and other troops aboard left Alexandria on June 2nd, and after a voyage, uneventful except for the news of the death of Lord Kitchener, reached Marseilles on June 8th. Early next morning the battalion disembarked, and immediately entrained on a troop-train for northern France. Most of the men were accommodated in trucks on which were the signs with which they were to become familiar later—"40 hommes ou 8 chevaux." In summer-time France is a beautiful country and, as the route lay along the Rhone valley, the scenery was magnificent.

After their many weary months in the desert, the troops felt like schoolboys on a holiday, and as the train passed through the towns they cheered the inhabitants who welcomed them in return. Four days rations were carried on the train which stopped at various places where hot water was obtained for the meals. During these halts, cigarettes, fruits, and flowers were pressed upon the men and the "entente" seemed very "cordiale." This most interesting journey lasted three days, and on the 11th June the 45th detrained at Bailleul.

The battalion at once marched off to billets in the roomy barns of farmhouses around Meteren. For the first time, the troops were associated with the French peasantry, of whom they were to see so much in later years; they soon adapted themselves to the new conditions and got on well with these hospitable French people. Most of the soldiers quickly picked up a few French words and managed to make themselves understood; but in any case, in the war zone, many of the French had learnt a little English. The digger's desire to air his knowledge of French often led to amusing incidents. On one occasion at Meteren, the brigade's French interpreter, who spoke faultless English, was going around the companies to assess the cost of billeting. He inquired in English from an orderly the direction of another company, and the orderly, observing that the interpreter was a Frenchman since he wore a French officer's uniform, replied in 'pidgin' English mixed with a few French words incorrectly pronounced. After listening for a few minutes to this very unintelligible reply, the interpreter at last impatiently exclaimed, "For God's sake man, speak English—if you can!"

Owing to the wet weather, the training was chiefly confined to route marching, bayonet fighting, grenade throwing, and lectures on such subjects as anti-gas measures. Steel helmets were issued for the first time as well as gas masks, a few box respirators being given to specialists, as there were not sufficient at this period for a complete issue.

The battalion soon had the honour of being inspected by three distinguished Generals. On June 19th General Plumer reviewed the brigade and favourably commented on the steadiness of the battalion. Two days later the companies were seen at work by General Birdwood; and on June 22nd, Sir Douglas Haig, the Commander-in-Chief of the British Armies in France, held a review, which resulted in two rather amusing incidents. During the general salute, when the rifles were "At the present," the order was given by the C.O. to "Stand at ease," instead of "slope arms," followed by "order arms" and then "stand at ease." Without a moment's hesitation, the whole battalion went through the proper drill movement as if it were accustomed to receiving orders in this fashion. This little unrehearsed incident spoke volumes for the steadiness and training of the battalion. In his inspection, Sir Douglais Haig asked nearly every man in "A" Company if he were a farmer, obviously not realising that, unfortunately, the greater part of the Australian people live in the capital cities and large country towns.

Leave to Bailleul, at this time a large and prosperous town, was much appreciated and it was at Meteren that the first leave to England commenced, then only of 7 days duration. Captain Howden and R. S. M. Tuson were the first to go and as the years went by, this "Blighty" holiday was looked forward to for months ahead. Except for the sound of the distant guns and the sight of so many soldiers, British, Australian, Canadian, New Zealand and French, it was hard to realise that a titanic struggle was being waged a few miles away. But the entire absence of able-bodied Frenchmen in civil occupations was most noticeable and the fields were tilled by old men, women and girls. These women reflected the spirit of France in the way they took the place of their men-folk who were fighting the enemy "pour la patrie."

It was anticipated that the battalion would soon go into the front line, so the C.O., Adjutant and Company Commanders visited the Armentieres sector which was held by the New Zealand Division. On July 2nd the order was suddenly received that the 45th had to march at three hours notice to Sailly-sur-Lys, preparatory to going into the front line in the Fleurbaix sector,

south of Armentieres. As it was a Sunday and no previous
warning of the move had been received, many of the men were
absent from their billets enjoying the quietness of a summer's
afternoon in the countryside whilst others had drifted to the
estaminets. A hurried search was made for these men and late
that afternoon the battalion marched off for Sailly-sur-Lys
which was 11 miles distant. The battalion soon learnt to dislike
Sundays, because it seemed that the so-called day of rest was the
most strenuous one of the week.

CHAPTER V.

THE BAPTISM OF FIRE AT FLEURBAIX.

On arrival at Sailly-sur-Lys the unit went into shell-wrecked
billets, and next morning an advanced party of one officer per
company, the snipers, Lewis gun section, and one n.c.o. per
platoon went up to the front line to become familiar with the
new sector. The remainder of the battalion moved up late on
the night of July 4th and relieved the 3rd Bn. The relief was
completed at 2 a.m. without any casualties, though the enemy
was shelling the approaches. The frontage held by the 45th
was 1300 yards and the trenches were not good. Owing to the
low-lying nature of the country, the defences had to be formed by
building up the parapet; if trenches were dug deeper than two
feet they would be untenable in winter owing to the soakage of
water.

As the unit had a big frontage, it was necessary to have the
four companies in the front line, but each company had one
platoon in support. Battalion Headquarters were situated in an
orchard at Croix les Cornex. It was summer-time and the
cherry trees were in full bearing, so the men soon found how
much risk they could safely take for the sake of filling a tin hat
with ripe cherries. Though the surrounding country was flat,
it looked quite pretty, with many green copses and flowering
hedges.

Trench warfare was at its height at this time and there
were all sorts of trench stores to be taken over. Trench maps,
defence schemes, trench log books and aeroplane photographs
had to be accounted for. One night the gas alarm sounded and
there was an absolute bedlam of noises from the various gas
alarms, bells, gongs and rattles which were placed at intervals

in the trenches.   As this was the battalion's first experience, there was unusual excitement.   Lt. Varley had a patrol in "No-man's Land" when the alarm went, and one of his men almost fainted thinking he had been gassed. In another company, two officers were discussing whether it was safe to remove their gas helmets when they were told that "all safe" had been ordered a quarter of an hour before.   This alarm proved to be a false one, but no chances were taken; and gas helmets or box respirators were always worn until it was ascertained that there was no danger.

During this period the German aviators were very active, and in order to minimise movement when hostile aircraft were overhead special sentries were posted with field glasses and whistles to give warning by pre-arranged signals of their approach.   The enemy's artillery was active but principally on the support lines, and his sniping and machine gun fire went on intermittently to which our men willingly retaliated.   Though this sector was considered a quiet one, the battalion during its week's stay had 5 other ranks killed and 7 other ranks wounded, chiefly from German trench mortar bombs.   These bombs, which weighed several pounds, had a very steep angle of descent with an erratic trajectory, and when the sentries heard the report of the firing they would warn the rest of the men who would dash for cover after watching the bomb hurling through mid-air. These trenches were infected with rats, and some of the men used to amuse themselves by putting cheese on the end of their bayonets and shooting as the rats reached the bait.

The supply of rations, stores and ammunition was comparatively easy in this sector which had two dumps, known as Dead Dog Dump and Tin Barn Dump, from which the rations, etc., were pushed up on trucks on a Decauville tram line almost up to the front trenches; but in other sectors communications were by no means so convenient.   Three communication trenches known as Devon Avenue, Dead Dog Avenue and Watling Street, which were long and winding, led to the support and front lines. It was here that the troops first used duckboards (sections of wooden foot-way) which played such an important part on the Western front in making trenches passable.

On July 11th the battalion's initiation into trench warfare in France came to an end and it was relieved by the 55th which, a week later, took part in the battle of Fromelles.   The 45th moved back to Sailly-sur-Lys and the next day marched to its former billets at Meteren.   These billets were very welcome, especially to those men who had been under fire for the first time. The battalion was not to remain here long however, for instructions were received that the 4th Division was to move to the Somme battlefield to take part in the great Allied offensive that had been going on since July 1st.

It was realised that the conditions down on the Somme would be very different from the trench warfare at Fleurbaix. There would be frequent moves and long marches, so it was essential that the battalion should be as mobile as possible. Orders were issued that all surplus baggage was to be stored, and a minute inspection was made of the men's packs. As the Officers were allowed to have valises weighing only 35 pounds, there were many heated arguments with the Q.M. who, however, was adamant in insisting on adhering to the regulations. The surplus stores and baggage, as well as the band instruments, were despatched to Thos. Cook & Sons, Boulogne, and were not seen for many months.

CHAPTER VI.

POZIERES.

Early on the morning of July 14th, the 45th entrained at Bailleul, and after a journey of several hours arrived at Doullens whence it marched to Berteaucourt, 15 miles distant. This was a difficult march as the men were carrying two blankets as well as their packs, rifles, etc., and had just finished an eight-hours train journey. A hot meal could not be obtained until the battalion had marched several miles, and the men soon showed the effects of marching on an empty stomach. Berteaucourt was reached that evening and the troops went into billets which had been allotted by the billeting party which had gone ahead.

This village, where the battalion remained for a fortnight, although it was under orders to move at short notice, was a large one and the billets were comfortable. Picardy is very beautiful in summer-time and the route marches through the neighbouring villages were enjoyable as well as being good training for the strenuous days which followed. Amongst other training, tactical exercises were carried out in the big wood at St. Ouen. At Berteaucourt the men made many friends with the French people who were sorry to see them depart, because they had witnessed so many battalions march gaily off to the Somme battles to return a few weeks later with many familiar faces missing.

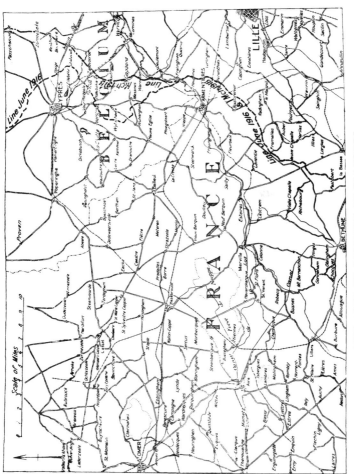

THE AREA OF FIGHTING IN FLANDERS.

On July 27th the 45th marched to Rubempre where Sgts. McIntyre and Adams were appointed to commissioned rank, the former becoming the signalling officer. Two days later the march was resumed and the battalion camped for the night at Vadencourt. Here it saw units of the 1st Division which had been in the thick of the fighting at Pozieres and were marching back to the rest area, many of them carrying spiked German helmets as souvenirs of their victory. At Vadencourt the packs and greatcoats were dumped, and on August 1st the battalion marched via Warloy to Albert where it bivouacked on the brickfields. From here could be seen the original German lines which the British had captured in the opening attack on July 1st. The famous leaning statue on the spire of the Albert Cathedral was a prominent landmark. This statue of the Virgin Mary clasping the Child in her arms had been displaced from its upright position, and there was a superstition current amongst the French people that when the statue fell, the war would end, and end disastrously for those who caused it to fall. As events turned out, the statue fell in 1918 when it was hit by a British shell after the Germans had captured Albert, but the war did not end for another six months and then it was the Germans who were defeated. So much for superstition!

Whilst the 45th was at the brickfields, many instructions were issued for the role it was expected to play. On August 4th a move forward was made to a bivouac area at Tara Hill, 2 miles north east of Albert. That night the 2nd Division captured the high ground east of Pozieres. This attack was preceded by a terrific bombardment and the sky, lit by the flashes of the guns and the bursting of shells, glowed like a red sunset in midsummer. All night long the guns roared and the watching troops wondered what it was like in an inferno like that. The final issues of battle equipment were made, and next morning an advanced party (including guides) was sent forward to the front line. It was understood that the 45th would not take over the line until next day, but before the guides had returned, orders were received that it was to go into the line that evening. The Adjutant went forward, located the advanced pary, and arranged for guides to meet the battalion which moved up to relieve the 17th, 18th and 20th Battalions on the evening of August 5th.

The route from Tara Hill was through a shallow approach-gully known as Sausage Valley which was congested with artillery and units going into the line and those coming out. So thick was the traffic that the platoons had to move in single file and in many places they had to halt whilst the big guns which were close to the road fired. To make the relief more difficult, the communication trenches were congested with wounded men of the 5th Brigade being evacuated and with the battalions which were being relieved. The sector which the battalion took over consisted of two main lines, O.G. 1 and O.G. 2 (i.e., "Old German trench No. 1 and No. 2") 1000 yards north east of Pozieres. O.G. 1 bore some resemblance to a continuous line, but O.G. 2 had been shelled so much, first by our own artillery and then by the enemy, that practically all signs of a trench system had been obliterated. The battalion front extended for 600 yards from Munster Alley to the Bapaume Road. "B" Company under Captain Knox was on the right, "C" under Captain Howden was in the centre and "D" under Major Chapman was on the left. "A" under Captain Perry was in close support, and Battalion Headquarters and the R.A.P. were in some old German dugouts half a mile S.E. of Pozieres. Both during the relief and afterwards, the enemy kept up a heavy strafe and, amongst many other casualties, Major Chapman, a popular and able officer, and Lieut. Draper were killed just after they had taken over.

All through the night the enemy kept up a heavy bombardment and, at 4.30 a.m. on the first morning, he made a counter-attack which our men easily repulsed with machine gun and rifle fire. Throughout the day he shelled the Pozieres ridge with H.E. and shrapnel and that afternoon Captain Knox with "B" Company rendered great assistance to a Yorkshire battalion on the right by co-operating in an attack on Munster Alley and capturing 30 prisoners. In this attack the battalion bombers under Lieut. Ferguson, C.S.M. Young, Sgts. Leddy and Gocher did excellent work. So severe was the enemy shelling that during the first 24 hours the battalion's casualties were 2 officers and 30 other ranks killed and 70 other ranks wounded. The continuous artillery fire made the evacuation of the wounded difficult matter and, besides our own heavy casualties, there were wounded men of the 2nd Division and some wounded Germans to be evacuated. Many of our men risked their lives in searching "No-man's Land" for wounded of the 2nd Division.

On the morning of August 7th the enemy made a strong attack in the vicinity of the Windmill (the stump of which lay near the O.G. lines) on the 48th Bn. which was on the left. This attack was broken up by a spirited counter-attack by the 48th and 14th Battalions and from the south of the Bapaume road our men used their Lewis guns effectively and captured 5 Germans. During that day, the enemy's artillery fire was on an unprecedented scale, and the battalion suffered heavily, losing 21 other ranks killed, and 3 officers and 67 other ranks wounded. As "C" and "D" Companies had had many casualties, they were relieved by "A." The intensity of the enemy's shelling scarcely slackened on August 8th and many casualties were again the result. Captain Drinkwater, a very efficient young officer, and 9 other ranks were killed and 83 other ranks were wounded.

Despite the heavy shelling, the troops in the line were well fed. This was due to the foresight of the Q.M.'s staff who had brought the cookers right up to Bn. H.Q. only 1000 yards from the front line. The Q.M. had been informed by the out-going units that it was impossible to bring them further than Sausage Valley, but this would have resulted in a long journey for the carrying parties. The cookers were dug in under a bank in front of Bn. H.Q. and the preparation of hot meals under the supervision of Sgt. Curtis was continued during the heaviest bombardment.

The battalion was in the front line three days and, during that time, besides beating off counter-attacks, it had improved the trenches to make them tenable. Owing to the hurricane of shell fire, it had been impossible to have a proper sleep. The stretcher bearers had worked continuously in bringing in the wounded to the R.A.P. where the calm bearing and untiring energy of the R.M.O. Captain Elwell evoked much admiration from the men. Runners, signallers and stretcher-bearers constantly ran the gauntlet of the enemy's barrage, and particularly fine work was done by Sgt. Simpson and his signallers in maintaining the telephone wires, which were very frequently cut by the enemy's shells. On August 8th the battalion was relieved by the 46th, and went back to a support line near Bn. H.Q. This did not mean a rest, however, as numerous working parties had to be provided for the digging of communication trenches which had been almost obliterated. Three days later it went back into reserve in Sausage Valley, between La Boiselle and Contalmaison, where it remained for two days. During these five days in support and reserve the battalion lost 4 other ranks killed and 59 other ranks wounded.

Early on the morning of August 14th, the battalion relieved the 46th in the front line where it remained for two days. Though the nights were quiet, in the daytime the enemy's shelling was severe and 12 other ranks were killed and 1 officer and 45 other ranks were wounded. Amongst those killed were Sgt. Slee, a splendid soldier who always considered the welfare of his men first, C.S.M. Bailey, Sgt. Tolmie, L/Cpl. Mulholland, and Privates McNaught and Thompson, all of whom had left Australia with the original 13th Bn. During the ten days that the battalion had been in the Pozieres sector, it had suffered heavily as is shown by the following casualties: 3 officers and 76 other ranks killed and 7 officers and 334 other ranks wounded. Though the casualties were very high, the wonder is to anybody who was there that they were not considerably greater. It was a gruelling experience to be subjected to a heavy and sustained bombardment; the physical and mental strain was stupendous; but owing to the battalion's magnificent stand at Pozieres, its reputation ever afterwards was assured.

On the evening of August 15th the 45th was relieved by the 5th Bn. and moved back to Albert for the night The next day it marched for Berteaucourt stopping en route at Warloy and at Herrisart. Between the latter place and Berteaucourt a distance of 12 miles, it rained continuously and, though everybody was very weary, not a man fell out. As they swung along with a steady stride, all were conscious of the fact that they were lucky to have survived one of the fiercest bombardments of the whole war. Berteaucourt was reached on August 19th, and the men were not disappointed in the hearty welcome given them by the French people. The next three days were spent in resting and in repairing the ravages of war. Platoons had to be reorganised, deficiencies in equipment made up; and the boots, especially, required attention.

A short rest at Berteaucourt was much appreciated, as the countryside was very beautiful with its quaint old villages and green woods; the fields were bright with yellow of ripening crops, the scarlet hue of poppies, and the vivid blue of cornflowers. It was hard to leave this lovely place for the Somme battlefield but on August 23rd, the battalion marched to Talmas. The next day it went to Rubempre, where Major-General Cox addressed the brigade and presented six officers and seven other ranks with congratulatory cards, which were an equivalent to a mention in divisional orders and generally meant that the recipients would in due course be awarded a decoration by higher authority. On August 26th the 45th marched to Vadencourt where it remained two days. A very successful concert was held here, and the next day a church parade at which General Birdwood presented the first two decorations awarded to members of the unit Military Medals won by Private Young, a stretcher-bearer and Private McFadden, a runner.

On August 28th, the battalion marched into billets in Albert, and next day relieved the 26th Bn. in the front line between the Pozieres Windmill and Mouquet Farm. "B" Company was in the firing line on a front of 600 yards, "A" Company in close support, and "C" and "D" in support. Before going into the line this time, Major Rowland had gone to the 12th Training Battalion in England; his place as second-in-command was filled by Major Lee who had been succeeded as Adjutant by Lieut. A. L. Varley.

The weather was by this time bad. It rained nearly all the time the battalion was in the line; but, though the mud was bad enough, it was nothing like that which was to be experienced in the months to come. On August 30th "D" Company took over the firing line as well as an extra 150 yards of front. The next day the 45th was relieved by the 2nd Canadian Bn., which had arrived for the first time on the Somme battlefield. During these two days the 45th had 1 other rank killed and 7 wounded. Though this relief took place in broad daylight, luckily there were no casualties, due, no doubt, to the fact that the German aeroplanes and observation balloons had suffered heavily from our airmen.

The next day the battalion moved back into support trenches S.E. of Ovillers-la-Boisselle which had been a German strong-point and the scene of some of the fiercest fighting early in July. On all sides were dead Germans, broken rifles, timber, rusty wire, and ammunition half buried in mud. On the night of September 1st a selected working party of 5 officers and 200 men under Captain Howden dug an assembly trench near Mouquet Farm for an attack which other brigades were to make. This trench was successfully excavated under great difficulties but 3 other ranks were wounded. The next day the battalion marched back to Albert and thence by stages through Warloy and Rubempre to Beauval, which was reached on September 6th. Whilst at Warloy, Sergeants Pickup, Pring, and Morrell were appointed to commissioned rank. At Beauval the battalion got ready for the move to the northern sector and the Wytschaete area, South of Ypres.

CHAPTER VII.

THE WYTSCHAETE SECTOR.

On September 8th the 45th detrained at Proven and marched to Victoria Camp near Reninghelst. This camp, which was partly hutted and the remainder tents, with duckboarded paths, etc., seemed almost luxurious after the forward zone on the Somme.

Training was at once resumed but was limited by the fact that the surrounding country was given over to the intense cultivation of hops, wheat, and potatoes. The troops found a big difference between the local inhabitants who were mostly Flemish, and the French in Picardy. Though the Flemish spoke better English than the French the men made friends quicker with the latter who were more hospitable and sympathetic. Whilst at this camp, General Cox presented congratulatory cards to 14 n.c.o.'s and men for their good work on the Somme.

Preparatory to going into the line half-way between Wytschaete and St. Eloi, the battalion moved to a very uncomfortable place called Ontario Camp near Rening Helst. Two days later on September 20th, it relieved the 50th Canadian Bn. in a support position at Ridgewood, north of Vierstraat. This was a pretty spot with comfortable sand-bagged shelters in a big wood; and as there was very little shelling, except for the necessity of providing numerous working parties it was a comparatively easy time.

On September 26th, the battalion moved into the front line, relieving the 47th on a frontage of 1000 yards, with two companies in the firing line, one in support, and one in reserve in the Bois Carre. In this sector the trench warfare was similar to that at Fleurbaix, with plenty of patrolling and erecting of barbed-wire entanglements at night, and the maintenance of the low-lying trenches in good order by constant repairs. Owing to the soil being unsuitable, the construction of deep dugouts similar to the German ones on the Somme was impossible. Trench warfare had by this time, become complicated and numerous "returns" had to be made out and signed and daily "intelligence summaries" circulated. The S.O.S. signal had to be known; this was to be used by the senior officer on the spot after he was certain that the enemy was concentrating in his front trenches for an attack or was actually attacking. At this particular period, the S.O.S. signal was the firing of a white aster rocket which was a sign for all available supporting artillery to put down a barrage in No-man's Land and on the front and support lines of the enemy.

Restrictions were placed on the use of the telephone for fear of the listening sets of the enemy or unauthorised persons picking up information. To prevent this, information that might be of use to the enemy, when telephoned, had to be sent in a special code. As it had been proved that spies had been operating in this part of the front the presence of any strangers was investigated. Also men were warned not to talk in estiminets about casualties and probable moves. The spy mania was at its height and many reports, especially about light signals at night, were found to be without foundation.

Whilst at Wytschaete, the battalion lost two fine sergeants: Sgt. Roscoe, an original 13th Bn. man, was killed whilst getting ready to leave for six months duty with the 12th Training Bn. and Sgt. Proctor, when about to proceed to the Cadet-Officer's School. At this period the 13th Bn. was on the immediate left flank—the first time since their arrival in France that the two battalions had been closely associated.

On October 2nd the 45th was relieved by the 47th and moved back into reserve; "C" Company went to Ridgewood, "D" Company to Vierstraat and the remainder of the Murrumbidgee Camp at La Clytte. This camp was very comfortable and hot baths and clean clothing were obtainable at the divisional baths. Only men who have fought and lived in the same clothes night and day for weeks at a time can appreciate the absolute luxury of a hot bath. The battalion was in reserve for 12 days and during this period, large working parties were supplied, chiefly for the building of Brigade Transport Lines. The bricks for the floors were brought each night from the ruins at Ypres which was only a few miles distant. Some of the men obtained souvenirs from the famous Cloth Hall which at this time was not quite demolished. Whilst here the strength of the battalion was augmented by the arrival of very fine reinforcements and by men returning from hospital.

When in reserve, a specially selected party, under Capt. Howden was trained for a raid, to take place when the 45th returned to the line, which it did on October 14th, relieving the 47th Bn. The next night, the raid directed by Capt. Howden was successfully carried out. The raiding party under Capt. L. Young entered the enemy's trenches in the Bois Quarante, and searched them for a distance of 100 yards, but the Germans had vacated them as soon as our artillery opened. However, some useful information was gathered about the enemy's front line. The details of the signalling communications, an important factor in raids, were carefully worked out by Sgt. Simpson. After the successful withdrawal of the raiding party, the enemy retaliated with artillery and trench mortar fire and five other ranks were wounded.

In this sector owing to the good communication trenches, it was possible for the rations, etc., to be sent up in the daylight. Whilst here, the band instruments were brought up from

Boulogne and the battalion band under Sgt. Coombes, was re-organised. The men soon became very proud of their band whose influence in assisting to maintain the morale of the unit in the strenuous months ahead was invaluable.

On October 15th, whilst the 45th was actually in the front line, the voting for the First Referendum—to decide whether Australia should resort to conscription for raising reinforcements—was held. There were many heated arguments for and against and it was evident that a fair proportion voted "No." Some said they did not want to have conscripted soldiers fighting alongside themselves who were volunteers; others thought Australia would suffer in many ways if all the fit men of fighting age were sent abroad, overlooking the fact that only sufficient men from certain categories would be called up failing volunteers to maintain a definite number of reinforcements each month. The Referendum, taken at the front and in Australia, resulted in the proposal being rejected by a narrow majority. As the war went on and reinforcements dwindled, many must have repented of their generous act in voting "No." The battalion went into the line and "over the top" time and time again, and upon each occasion men were killed or wounded; yet, if a constant stream of reinforcements had been kept up, those men who had left Australia from 1914 to 1916 could have been given a well-earned rest.

On October 18th at Murrumbidgee Camp, nine other ranks were presented with Military Medals by General Birdwood. Four days later the battalion was relieved by a battalion of the Kings Royal Rifle Corps and moved back to Victoria Camp near Reninghelst. During the whole period in which the 45th was in the Wytschaete sector, 7 other ranks were killed and 18 wounded. Even in the quietest part of the line, casualties were inevitable.

The stay at Victoria Camp was spent in refitting and getting ready for the next move. Here 3 officers and 4 other ranks received congratulatory cards from the Divisional Commander. On October 26th the battalion marched to Godevaersvelde and entrained for Amiens. The next day it arrived at Longpre and marched to billets at Brucamps. The 45th was once more on the Somme, where it was to endure the hardships and sufferings of that never-to-forgotten winter of 1916-1917.

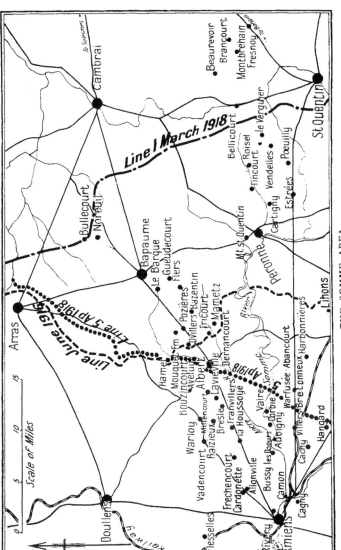

THE SOMME AREA.

CHAPTER VIII.

ON THE SOMME IN THE WINTER OF 1916-1917 *AND STORMY TRENCH.*

After its arrival from the north, the battalion stayed several days at Brucamps, a dirty little village seven miles north of Amiens. Whilst here 100 reinforcements were taken on strength. On November 1st the battalion marched to Vignacourt where more comfortable billets were found. In this part of France, the peasants do not live in farmhouses on their farms, but in villages from which they go out daily to work in their fields. The villages are very similar, with the farmhouses usually built in the form of a quadrangle, the dwelling house, barn, stable, etc., forming the four sides. In the centre of the quadrangle is the "middin" or manure heap, which is greatly valued by the peasant as he uses it to fertilise his fields. The well, from which the water for drinking, etc., is obtained, was generally in the quadrangle, often in close proximity to the "middin." Owing to the danger of infection, every precaution was taken by the military authorities to prevent the troops from drinking this water unless it had been first boiled or otherwise purified. The interior of the houses are scrupulously clean but it was always a source of wonder that the local inhabitants, living so close to these manure heaps and drinking the water straight from the wells, did not contract typhoid fever or some other disease. It was said of the peasants of Vignacourt that when chloride of lime was placed on the "middins," they complained that it affected their water supply in the wells!

The next day the battalion marched to Vaux-en-Amienois, where it spent several days during which time the men were issued with sheep-skin vests in anticipation of the cold weather to come. On November 8th, the 45th was for the first time transported by motor-bus. These buses belonged to a French mechanical transport company and everybody agreed that it was infinitely better than "foot-slogging." The immediate destination was Dernancourt and this journey took only five hours whereas, by march route, it would have taken two days solid marching. Not only was time thus saved, but the troops avoided much fatigue, and there is no doubt that greater use of motor buses and motor lorries for the transportation of infantry would have considerably increased their fighting efficiency. This fact was realised in the last year of the war, when motor transport of infantry was largely used.

The men with one accord gave Dernancourt first place for extreme filthiness and discomfort. The weather was rapidly becoming worse, and the surrounding country resembled a morass. At this place 2 officers and 8 other ranks were presented with congratulatory cards for their good work in the Wytschaete sector. On November 11th the battalion marched to Fricourt east of Albert where there was a good hutted camp.

The brigade was to go into the line near Gueudecourt and the next day the 45th marched to Bernafay Wood, where it became the reserve battalion in anticipation of an attack it was intended it should carry out. Except for a few trench shelters the troops had only their waterproof ground sheets and greatcoats to protect them from the elements to which had been added a fifth, mud. Away from the limited bivouac site and the few roads, the countryside was a sea of mud. The ground had been ploughed up by the British and German shells in the fierce fighting for this position in the previous July, and all that remained of a once beautiful wood were a few gaunt trees and stumps. The amount of traffic was stupendous. The road near Bernafay Wood was thick with motor lorries, motor cars, ambulance and G.S. wagons, guns and ammunition limbers, mules, horses and men. In the road itself were large shell-holes full of water and mud, and it was no unusual sight to see a mule or limbered G.S. wagon half disappear in one of them. The regimental transport, which was at Pommier Redoubt, had a herculean task in bringing up stores and rations to the battalion.

On the day the brigade went into the line, General Glasfurd was mortally wounded when reconnoitring the front sector. His death was a great loss to the Brigade and to the whole A.I.F. His courage, unselfishness, and devotion to duty were an inspiration to all ranks under his command. Lieut.-Colonel Herring temporarily assumed command of the brigade until the new Commander, Brigadier General C. Robertson, was appointed.

Whilst in reserve the battalion was used for working parties, principally in road-making. Here for the first time saw that famous all-British invention, the Tank. Nearby, several derelict tanks, which had been used in the capture of Flers, were objects of great curiosity on account of their weird shape and reputed capabilities. On November 18th and 19th, the battalion relieved the 46th in the front line near Gueudecourt. Two companies were in the firing line and two in support. The front trenches, known as Grease Trench and Goodwin's Trench, were in a bad state, wet and muddy, with only a few short sections duck-boarded.

So bad was the condition of the front line, that every 48 hours the two support companies relieved the front line companies. More frequent relief was out of the question, owing to the extreme fatigue caused by moving up through the almost impassable communication trenches. Indescribable discomfort due to the rain and mud, frost and snow, was suffered by the troops. Strenuous efforts were made to alleviate their misery by hot meals and dry socks, brought up nightly from the transport lines. "Tommy Cookers" were distributed so that the men could make hot drinks in the front line, and every morning at "stand down" a tot of rum was issued. Rum was sent to the line in stone demijohns, on which were letters, "S.R.D." It was wittily but untruthfully said that they meant, "Seldom Reaches Destination."

During the eight days the battalion was in the line, the enemy's artillery was active, and every night frequent patrols were sent out. On one occasion, a patrol captured one German and killed three others. Whilst in the line, here, Lieut. Dolton and 7 other ranks were killed, and one officer and 28 other ranks wounded. Owing to the extreme cold and continuous standing in wet trenches, many men were evacuated to hospital with trench feet. In order to keep this much dreaded complaint down to a minimum, the men wore gum boots and were compelled to rub their feet with whale oil under the supervision of section and platoon commanders.

On November 27th the battalion was relieved by the 13th and moved back to New Charlton Camp at Bazentin. Most of the camps in this area were built of Nissen huts, semi-cylindrical in shape and made of galvanised iron lined with wood. Easily transported and erected, these huts were a great boon to the troops in winter. Whilst here the battalion was employed in making roads, unloading artillery ammunition, and constructing a light "Decauville" railway line. At this camp, information was received that three M.C.'s and 4 D.C.M.'s had been awarded to the battalion.

A week later the 45th less "A" and "B" Companies, which remained behind to supply working parties, entrained at Quarry Siding for Meaulte whence it went back to Dernancourt. Though the weather was bad, training was resumed. Whilst here Sergeants Kirman and Simpson were appointed to commissioned ranks, and three other ranks were awarded the Military Medal.

On December 17th the battalion, less the two companies, entrained at Edgehill for Flesselles, the transport going by road. Here it settled down for a rest and to spent Christmas. Training was not neglected, especially musketry. Owing to the numerous casualties in the last four months there were rapid promotions amongst the non-commissioned officers in whose training the strong characters of R.S.M. Tuson and C.S.M. Young had a very fine influence. In order to keep the men fit, route marches through the surrounding country were made. Recognition of the good work in the line was made by the presentation to 2 officers and 7 other ranks of the Divisional Commander's congratulatory card.

Christmas Day was spent at Flesselles, and for the Christmas dinner the ordinary ration was supplemented by the purchase of certain delicacies; in addition, each man received a parcel from the battalion Comforts Fund, containing such things as pipes, tobacco, cigarettes, sweets and socks. These simple gifts had a special significance to soldiers fighting thousands of miles away from their own folk, and they were valued because they had been packed with loving care and the best of good wishes. On Boxing Day "A" and "B" Companies, which had been working very hard in the forward area, rejoined the battalion for a few days before the next move was made. Whilst at Flesselles leave was given to 50 men daily to visit Amiens, which was only six miles away, and which at that time was full of French civilians and Allied soldiers.

On December 30th, Major General Cox said farewell to the brigade. He had made himself very popular with the whole division, and his influence in the first nine months of its existence had a far-reaching effect in making the 4th Division the efficient fighting formation that it always was. His successor was Major-General Holmes, from the 5th Infantry Brigade, who had commanded the Naval and Military Expeditionary Force which captured German New Guinea in 1914.

On New Year's Day, 1917, the battalion held a very successful sports meeting in which the running and jumping events and the platoon drill and company cooker competitions, were keenly contested. R.Q.M.S. Neaves, who had been appointed to commissioned rank, became Quartermaster, and C.Q.M.S. Sorrell was promoted to be R.Q.M.S. The position of Transport Officer was filled by Lieut. Morrell. On January 2nd the battalion was on the move once more. This time it marched to Franvillers and the next day reached Dernancourt. On January 5th it moved to Fricourt and on the 6th to Bazentin. That afternoon two companies went forward to the front area where they relieved two companies of the 1st Bn. in Bull's Run and Pilgrims Way which were support trenches near Flers. The next day the remainder of the battalion moved forward and two companies relieved two companies of the 1st Bn. in the front line near Gueudecourt.

The trenches here were in a very bad state and much work had to be done, especially to the main communication trench, Eve Alley. In this trench the mud and slush were over the men's knees the whole way; rather than wade through it, the majority preferred to risk walking on top and being sniped at by rifle fire or hit by machine gun or artillery fire. The relief of the front line companies was so fatiguing that it was decided that they should change over only once every four days. The weather was much colder with heavy falls of snow; the frosts, too, were so severe that the water in the shell holes was frozen for several inches. The mud began to freeze and horses and vehicles would crash through the frozen crust on the surface and become bogged in the soft mud underneath. At the horse lines the troughs froze, and water was obtained for cooking purposes by filling sandbags with blocks of ice. With the advent of this bitterly cold weather, the sick parades, due to exposure and hardships in the front line, grew very large. To prevent this abnormal wastage of men to hospital, a rest station was established at the Regimental Aid Post, where the least serious cases were nursed back to health.

During the ten days in the front line, 7 other ranks were killed and 20 wounded. On January 15th the two front line companies were relieved by the 46th Bn. prior to which a German raiding party, about 50 strong tried to raid one of our posts but was driven off with heavy casualties. The next day the remainder of the battalion was relieved. On relief the battalion moved into support in Gap and Switch Trenches and on the day after that, went back to Mametz Camp. This was a comfortable place and as each hut had a couple of braziers, the men used to augment their daily issue of fuel by bartering rum and cigarettes for supplies from the Tommy sentries on the coal dump at the railway siding. Whilst at Mametz numerous working parties had to be sent out. Full use was made of the divisional baths at Fricourt, and the opportunity was taken to disinfect the blankets and uniforms, as it had been proved that lice were responsible for disseminating trench fever.

Whilst here during the absence on leave of the Brigade Commander, Lieut.-Colonel Herring again temporarily took charge of the Brigade, and as Major Lee had been seconded for

Staff work, Major Perry, who was now second-in-command, took command of the battalion for the time. In the New Year's Honours List the D.S.O. had been awarded to Colonel Herring, and 4 officers and 4 other ranks were mentioned in despatches.

On Feb. 8th, the 45th moved forward to a support position in Gap and Switch Trenches and relieved the 14th Bn. Here the unit was engaged in digging trenches and erecting wire entanglements; also in carrying duck-boards for the trenches, and for the tracks by which the muddy wastes were rendered passable. Eight days later, it began to take over from the 46th Bn. in Pilgrim's Way and on February 17th it went into line in Stormy Trench. Grease Trench, farther back, had previously been the front line, but Stormy Trench had been captured some days before by the 13th Bn. in an attack in which the hero of the 13th, Captain Murray, won the V.C. In retaliation for this recent "stunt," the German artillery and trench mortar fire was very active. Every night patrols were sent out to the block that had been established on the left flank of Stormy Trench and to inspect the enemy's wire entanglements in anticipation of a projected raid by the battalion.

On February 19th, orders were issued to the 45th to capture that portion of Stormy Trench still held by the enemy beyond the block. The attack was to be made on the evening of February 20th by the party that had been selected for the raid, but owing to a sudden thaw that set in at midday and the constant traffic in connection with the supply of bombs and ammunition, the trenches had become so churned up that they were practically impassable. Captain Howden, in charge of the attacking party, after a thorough reconnaisance recommended that, owing to the condition of the mud and the consequent temporary exhaustion of the men, the attack should be postponed. Lieut.-Colonel Herring made a recommendation to this effect to Brigade Headquarters which, as arrangements had been made with the artillery for its co-operation, sent Major Lee (then attached to the Brigade Staff) to inspect the front line. His appreciation confirmed absolutely the report of the battalion, and it was decided to postpone the attack until the next day.

In the early hours of February 21st, the attacking party of the 45th Bn. captured the position. This party which was not supported by artillery, was a small one, consisting of Captain Howden, Lieutenants Cornish and R.A.M. Murray and specially selected parties of bombers and Lewis gunners. The attackers assembled in adjacent shell holes and by a concerted movement, rushed the trench under cover of machine gun and trench mortar fire. The Germans at this point were taken by surprise, and quickly surrendered. The attacking party then bombed its way along the trench and either killed or drove before them those who did not surrender. Owing to the muddy state of the lines, progress was slow, and though rifle grenades were used, the resistance soon stiffened. After capturing 300 yards the attackers established an effective block at the end of the trench. Just before dawn, an enemy counter attack was driven off. Altogether some 30 Germans were killed, and 50 wounded and the prisoners captured were 21 unwounded and 8 wounded Germans. The only casualties suffered by the battalion were 1 officer and 7 other ranks slightly wounded. The unqualified success of this minor operation was due to the preliminary arrangements, the detailed reconnaisance by the leaders beforehand, and the magnificent dash shown by all ranks in the attack. Special credit was due to Capt. Howden, whose accurate appreciation on the previous night undoubtedly saved what was a brilliant little victory from being a regrettable incident.

On the night of February 22nd, the battalion followed up this success with a further attack. Captain Howden was again O.C. attacking party, which consisted of Lieutenants Ferguson and Muir, two bombing sections, and an escort of Lewis gunners, assisted by a bomb-carrying party under C.S.M. Crooks. Under cover of a Stokes Mortar barrage, the party, led by Lieut. Ferguson, successfully rushed the enemy's block. They then bombed their way along the trench for 150 yards and captured one trench mortar and 32 prisoners, for whose capture C.S.M. Crooks was largely responsible. Crooks, when he came to a German dug out, would demand: "Any Fritzes down there?" and by his humorous remarks held his men together. The captured trench was then consolidated by a party under Captain Schadel, who when out in "No-Man's Land" dispersed with his revolver a German patrol. The attacking party had three men wounded, but besides the capture of the prisoners they killed and wounded many Germans. One of the prisoners, a German cadet-officer and ex-Oxford student, who spoke excellent English, indignantly complained to Battalion Headquarters that one Australian in the attacking party had jumped on him and rudely said, "Tick Tick," meaning that he should hand over his watch.

These two minor operations, in which 450 yards of trenches and 61 prisoners were captured with slight losses to the battalion, showed that the morale of the unit was very high even though it was enduring an extremely severe winter under the worst conditions. During the 16 days that it had been in the line, the casualties, including those incurred in the recent "stunts," were as follows:—Lieut. Meggitt, whilst acting as Brigade Bombing Officer, and 18 other ranks were killed, and 2 officers and 82 other ranks were wounded. Most of these casualties occurred during the heavy bombardment that the enemy put down on February 13th.

Shortly after the capture of Stormy Trench the Germans commenced their long premeditated retirement to the Hindenburg Line, but the 4th Division was not at first called upon to follow it up, being sent to the rear for rest and training. On February 29th the battalion was relieved in the front line by the 58th Bn., and moved back to Mametz Camp. The troops during the last two months had undergone a very severe mental and physical strain. Many were suffering from exposure to the extreme cold, and nearly all had swollen feet from standing in the icy slush and mud. Three days later the unit moved to a comfortable camp at Becourt, preparatory to going to the rest area. During nearly the whole of the four previous months it had been in the forward area during a winter that was one of the most severe in France for 50 years, and in that time those troops suffered hardships which they can never forget.

CHAPTER IX.

BULLECOURT AND A WELL-EARNED REST AT BRESLE.

It was on March 1st that the battalion marched back out of the line to rest billets. Some much-needed reorganisation was carried out, and the mornings were devoted to training which consisted chiefly of route marches, or else of lectures and specialist training given indoors owing to the inclemency of the weather. In the afternoons, organised games were held and, as an indication of the good feeling which always existed between the officers and men, a football match between the officers and other ranks was played. Whilst at Becourt C.S.M. Young and Sergeants Leddy and Maiden were appointed to commissioned rank. As soon as the battalion got back to Bresle, the officers started a Mess as also did the Sergeants. It was thhe first time this had been possible since leaving Egypt, and the change was greatly appreciated as Mess life does much to promote goodfellowship among fellow-members. It enabled both officers and

Lt.-Col. S. L. PERRY, D.S.O., M.C.

sergeants to get to know better those who had in the recent months joined their ranks. On March 23rd the battalion moved forward to Shelter Wood camp, near Fricourt. Here Lt. Colonel Herring took command of the brigade during the temporary absence of the Brigadier, and Major Perry commanded the Battalion.

Mention has already been made of the first stage of the German retirement from the Somme battlefield in the early months of 1917. This was due to the belief of the enemy that, owing to the repeated onslaughts of the Allies in the First Battle of the Somme, the German line in this part would be untenable if the Allies continued the offensive in the spring. To avoid this the Germans withdrew gradually to the Hindenburg Line which had been feverishly prepared during the winter. At this time the Australian troops in the line were the 2nd and 5th Divisions which vigorously followed up the retiring enemy and captured Bapaume. These two divisions were relieved by the 1st and 4th Divisions just before the enemy reached his famous line.

On March 28th, the 45th went forward to a tented camp at Le Barque near the well-known Butte de Warlencourt. On the way up it passed through Pozieres, a place very different from that in those strenuous days in August. Scattered about were the graves of our dead over which the battalion pioneers had erected simple white wooden crosses; the sight of these brought back poignant memories of the sacrifices and bitter struggle on the Pozieres Ridge.

Bapaume, which had been mined by the Germans before they left it, was on fire and many explosions occurred causing casualities to the Australians who first entered it. For several days the battalion was engaged in salvage work in this town, and in repairing the main road in which were huge mine craters. Whilst at Le Barque, the following awards were announced for the magnificent work done at Stormy Trench and during that period: One bar to the M.C.; four M.C.'s; one D.C.M.; one bar to the D.C.M. and thirty-one M.M.'s This was a unique list as it meant that on this occasion a decoration had been awarded for every recommendation made by the C.O.

On April 2nd, the battalion moved forward to the northern outskirts of Bapaume. Its strength had been greatly increased by the arrival of numerous reinforcements from the 4th Divisional Base Depot, at Etaples. Preparations were now being made for the forthcoming attack on the Hindenburg Line near Bullecourt, and officers and n.c.o.'s reconnoitred the line which the brigade was to take over. On April 7th, the 4th and 12th Infantry Brigades relieved the 13th Brigade which had recently captured Noreuil. These two, in conjunction with a British division on the left, were to break the redoubtable Hindenburg Line at Bullecourt and allow the Cavalry to pass through. This attack and another one at Arras where the British had already had a wonderful success, were to be a smashing blow to the enemy.

On the 12th Brigade sector, the attack was to be made by the 46th and 48th Bns., with the 47th in support and 45th in reserve. On April 9th, the 51st relieved the 46th and 48th which during their two days in the line had found the barbed wire to have been practically undamaged by our artillery. The attack was to have taken place on the morning of April 10th, but, owing to unforseen difficulties, the tanks, which were to be used in large numbers, could not get into position in time. Accordingly, the assault was postponed until the next day. At 4.30 a.m. on April 11th, the 46th and 48th advanced from the jumping off trenches, following closely the few tanks that had arrived in time or which were not disabled early in the attack by the enemy's artillery. The enemy's first belt of wire was found to have been broken by shells, sufficiently at any rate to enable most of the troops to get through with some difficulty, and under sharp fire. Notwithstanding their heavy casualties these two battalions very gallantly continued their advance, the 46th capturing the first objective at 5.50 a.m. and the 48th Bn. the second, through uncut wire at 6.20 a.m. They were soon counter-attacked but were reinforced by portion of the 47th Bn. Owing to defective communications, they could not be effectively supported by our artillery, and these two sorely-tried battalions, greatly weakened by casualties, and fiercely counter-attacked from front and flanks, were forced to withdraw to the original front line. In a similar way, the 4th Infantry Brigade after getting its objective had been forced to withdraw under pressure of a terrific counter-attack. The failure of this attack was due to its lack of surprise and to the failure of the Tanks to play the part expected of them. In this heroic but tragic battle of Bullecourt the 12th Infantry Brigade has casualties amounting to 30 officers and 900 other ranks.

On the morning of April 11th, the 45th Bn. marched to Noreuil and by midnight had taken over the old front line behind which the other battalions had been withdrawn. The situation was still very obscure. Advanced posts were established by the two companies in the front line, and active patrolling was carried out lest the enemy should follow on with another counter-attack. The 45th was kept very busy in bringing in the killed and the numerous wounded of the day before. It remained in the line for three days, during which time 7 other ranks were killed and 40 other ranks were wounded. On the night of April 13th, it was relieved and moved back to Bapaume where it entrained for Albert. From here it went to a camp at Shelter Wood at Fricourt and four days later was back at its old billets at Bresle.

After its long period of trench warfare, the unit settled down to solid training in all its phases up to battalion training. "A" Company was inspected by General Gough, the Army Commander, at its training, and was complimented for its very fine work. In order to learn the latest ideas during the whole time the battalion was in France, selected officers and n.c.o.'s and men were continually sent to Divisional, Corps and Army Schools of Instruction for courses in infantry training, rifle and bayonet, Lewis gun work, signalling, bombing, and anti-gas measures. These courses were of the greatest value as officers and others were trained as instructors and brought back the latest methods thereby helping to maintain the high standard for which the Australians were noted. The supply of officers was maintained by specially selected warrant and non-commissioned officers being sent to the Officer-Cadet Battalions which the War Office had established at famous colleges at Oxford and Cambridge. After several months training they returned to the battalion as commissioned officers.

In order to train the reinforcements in England in the latest methods of warfare evolved in France, selected officers and n.c.o.'s were sent periodically for six months' duty with the 12th Training Bn. on Salisbury Plains. On arrival from Australia, the reinforcements for the four battalions of the brigade were drafted into this training battalion. After several months training there, these reinforcements with the men returning to duty from hospitals in England were sent to the 4th Divisional Base Depot, at Etaples, in France. Here they were put through a quick concentrated course at the training ground, commonly known as the "Bull Ring," and were sent up to their battalions as required. Soon after its arrival in France, the battalion's own reinforcements (known as the 1st, 2nd, etc., Reinforcements, 45th Bn.) had begun to arrive.

With the approach of spring the weather greatly improved and the landscape became beautiful again with green trees and grass, and the hedges and wildflowers were in bloom. Brighter surroundings and a good rest soon raised the spirits of the troops and they began to look back on the winter campaign as a hideous dream. On April 25th, Brigade sports were held at Henencourt Wood to commemorate Anzac Day, and, though the competition between the battalions was keen, "A" Company won the silver cup for the best drill-squad in the brigade. In a Divisional Musketry Competition which was held to raise the standard of musketry and to promote friendly rivalry between the various units, the 45th put up a creditable performance. A Brigade Transport show was also held, and this had the effect of bringing the regimental transport up to a state of excellence that it had never reached before.

Various entertainments were held for the troops including concerts by "The Anzac Coves" and "The Smart Set," the latter being a concert party of the 4th Division in which were several men from the battalion. These concerts were always much appreciated as also were the boxing contests held in a very big shed at Bresle. On May 12th the Division was inspected by General Birdwood, who presented 12 Military Medals to members of the battalion.

On May 12th, after a well-deserved rest for a month, the 45th marched to Dogsleg Huts, Bouzincourt, and the next day went to Aveluy, where it entrained for Bailleul and the northern sector. It had been in the Somme area for six months, and for the greater part of that time in the front line or the forward area.

CHAPTER X.

THE BATTLE OF MESSINES.

On May 16th the 45th arrived at Bailleul where it was billeted for the night. The next day, with the exception of "B" Company which was conveyed by buses to Dou Dou Farm, it marched to Neuve Eglise. Here it was engaged in unloading ammunition and whilst working on the dumps which were shelled by the enemy, 4 other ranks were killed and 16 wounded.

After a fortnight, the battalion was concentrated at Kortypyp Lines near Neuve Eglise where it spent six days in getting ready for the coming offensive at Messines. Officers and n.c.o.'s daily reconnoitred the approaches to the front line and the whole battalion inspected a large relief model of the position to be attacked. The great offensive had been under consideration by

General Plumer for over a year and the details had been worked out in great detail by his staff. The attack was to be made by Second Anzac Corps (which at that time comprised the New Zealand, 3rd and 4th Australian, and 25th British Divisions), in conjunction with the IX. and X. British Corps.

On June 7th, the Second Army attacked and captured the Messines-Wytschaete Ridge, which since 1914, had formed a big re-entrant in our line. Zero hour was 3.10 a.m. and the attack was preceded by the explosion of nineteen huge mines which had been prepared by tunnelling companies for months past. These terrific explosions did a lot of damage to the enemy's defences and badly shook his morale. At the same time the bombardment of his trenches, which had been going on intermittently for weeks increased to stupendous proportions. The 3rd Division, which was the right of II. Anzac and of the whole attack, captured the trenches between Ploegsteert Wood and Warneton; the New Zealand Division in the centre of the Corps captured Messines with the 25th British Division on its left and the IX Corps took Wytschaete. The divisions, which went over the top at zero hour, when the enemy was demoralised, had a sweeping victory. The attack of the 4th Division was more difficult. It had to pass through the New Zealand and 25th Divisions some twelve hours after zero and capture the final objective in broad daylight. This attack was to be made by the 12th and 13th Infantry Brigades on the right and left respectively. In the former Brigade's sector it was to be carried out by the 47th Bn. on the right and the 45th Bn. on the left.

The objective of the 45th was two lines of trenches known as Owl Support and Owl Trench which were 250 yards apart; and between this objective and the line reached by the New Zealanders was a strong point called Oxygen Trench. These trenches were strongly wired along the whole battalion front which was 750 yards in extent. The complete battalion was used in this attack, two companies to take the first line of trenches and the other two were to go through them in "leap-frog" fashion on to the second. "A" Company was to capture Oxygen Trench and the right of Owl Trench, and "C" Company was to take the left half. "B" and "D" Companies were to pass through the first two companies, and capture the right and left halves of Owl Support respectively.

On the morning of June 7th the battalion left Kortypyp Camp and marched by platoons along defined routes to Stinking Farm, north of Hill 63. At 11.30 a.m. it formed up in what had been No-Man's-Land the night before, and moved off in artillery formation to the jumping off line, east of Messines and just in rear of the advanced line of posts established by the New Zealanders that morning. At noon the order was received that zero hour which was to have been 1.10 p.m. was to be postponed for two hours to synchronise with an attack by a British Division north of Wytschaete. This enforced delay was most unfortunate as the battalion was well over the crest of Messines Ridge, and in full view of the enemy whose enfilade fire from the direction of Warneton caused casualties. Also, this delay gave the enemy warning of the attack and more time to bring up his reserves. Half an hour before the new zero, the battalion formed up on the jumping-off tape-line which had been gallantly laid out by Lieut. R. A. M. Murray, Cpl. Kingsley and Cpl. Kelly, the two former being killed just after they had completed their task. The enemy in readiness for his counter-attack began to put down a heavy barrage.

At the new zero hour, 3.10 p.m., the battalion moved off in artillery formation, though suffering heavily from shell fire, advanced steadily on its objective. Oxygen Trench was taken, but strong opposition was met all along Owl Trench, especially from a strong point in the form of a concrete "pill box" in the left half. Owing to the heavy machine gun fire from this point, "A" and "B" Companies went to the right, and "C" and "D" Companies deviated to the left. The right flank of the two right companies was in contact with the 47th Bn., but both flanks of the two left Companies were in the air. The command of these two companies rested with Capt. W. L. Young, M.C., who, though wounded early in the advance, very gallantly continued to direct it personally until he was killed just before the companies reached their objective.

"A" and "B" Companies on the right gained both objectives and captured 120 prisoners and two machine guns; but on the left only the first objective, Owl Trench, was taken. The few tanks that had co-operated had gone back before the final objective could be completely taken. Meanwhile the enemy had prepared his counter-attack which was launched in great force at 5 p.m. This was driven off except on the left flank where the two isolated companies, greatly reduced in strength by casualties, practically without officers or senior n.c.o.'s, and with both flanks in the air, were forced to retire to their jumping-off line. These two companies had suffered severly, as in "C" Company every officer had been killed, and in "D" all officers had been either killed or wounded. Owing to a grave misunderstanding, when it was observed that the enemy attack on the left flank had been successful, our artillery put down a barrage at 7.30 p.m. right along the battalion frontage in front of the jumping-off line. This cut off "A" and "B" Companies in Owl Trench and Owl Support and they suffered many casualties from our own artillery with whom they were unable to communicate. Meanwhile the enemy had counter-attacked again very heavily and these two companies, attacked from the front and the flanks and shelled from the rear, were forced to retire in conjunction with the left flank of the 47th Bn. to the jumping-off line. It was with bitter thoughts that they thus relinquished, through no fault of their own, the objective so gallantly captured that afternoon.

During the night the sadly-depleted battalion was reorganised and reinforced by two companies of the 48th Bn. and, at 8.30 a.m. next morning, it attacked and captured Owl Trench and Owl Support. The fierce fighting in this series of attacks and counter-attacks showed the superb qualities of the men, who were gallantly led by Captain A. S. Allen, ably assisted by Lieut. McIntyre and 2nd Lieuts. Muir and J. Young. The splendid co-operation of the two companies of the 48th Bn. with the depleted companies of the battalion was invaluable in this counter-attack. From 2 p.m. until 11 p.m. on June 8th, the whole battalion front was subjected to a heavy bombardment by the enemy who made another counter-attack at 7.30 p.m., but was driven off with losses. Later that night, a patrol under Lieut. McIntyre gained contact with the 51st Bn. on the left.

On the afternoon of June 9th, a bombing attack was made on the extreme left of Owl Support from which the enemy had not been completely dislodged the day before. Some 200 yards of trench was gained but further progress was blocked by two concrete "pill-boxes." Whilst gallantly leading his men in an attack on these, Lieut. Barton, who had a few weeks returned from the Cadet-Officer School, was killed. On the night of June 9th, the two companies of the 48th Bn. were relieved by the 46th which took over the line between the 47th and 45th. That night a fighting patrol under 2nd Lieut. Muir gained some useful information in the direction of Gapaard Farm. On the same night, two platoons made a successful attack on the left, in conjunction with the battalion on that flank. The artillery had done very little damage to the "pill-boxes" and the attacking platoons suffered heavily from machine gun fire and bombs. Amongst others killed was the leader, Lieut. McIntyre, a very popular and able officer who had shown conspicuous gallantry during the whole operations.

On June 11th the battalion was relieved and moved back to
the subsidiary line, near La Plus Douve Farm. It had played
a brilliant part in the Messines offensive, but during those four
days had suffered heavily, its casualties being 3 officers and 146
other ranks killed and 7 officers and 344 other ranks wounded.
Besides the officers who have already been mentioned, the following were amongst those killed: Lieut. H. B. Allen, a splendid
officer who had been acting as Brigade Bombing Officer; Lieut.
E. Garling, a capable and popular officer; 2nd Lieuts. Gocher and
C. E. Ryan, who had been promoted recently for fine leadership;
and Lieut. J. M. Swann, a recent reinforcement officer. Of all
the company officers who took part only two survived untouched.
This threw extra responsibility on the n.c.o.'s who also had suffered heavily, and they responded magnificently. Taking it as
a whole the battle of Messines was a great victory, but the 12th
and 13th Infantry Brigades would have had far less casualties,
and would have gained their objectives much more easily had
the zero hour been at 1.10 p.m. as originally intended and not
postponed until 3.10 p.m. This delay of two hours made all
the difference between an easy victory and a hard-fought success, as it gave the enemy time to recover from his demoralised
condition to meet the attack of the 4th Division, and to bring
up fresh troops for his strong counter-attacks.

On the night of June 12th the 45th marched back to la
Creche where it spent several days in resting and in obtaining
hot baths and clean clothing at Steenwerck. Here the "nucleus"
which had been left behind at Morbecque rejoined the battalion.
This "nucleus" consisted of small proportion of officers, n.c.o.'s
and specialists who had been left out of the attack, so that, in
case of heavy casualties, the battalion would have a nucleus of
trained personnel to build up the battalion again.   This pro-
cedure was followed throughout the remainder of the war, a different nucleus being left out of battle each time. Whilst at la
Creche the battalion was inspected by the Second Anzac Corps
Commander, General Godley, who expressed his admiration for
its fine achievements in the recent fighting.

On June 17th the battalion marched to Bailleul where it
embussed for Renescure. The few days spent here were much
appreciated as the countryside with its fields of growing crops
was looking beautiful. The battalion completed its refitting and
on June 17th it moved by bus to Doullieu where it was billeted
in scattered farmhouses. On June 26th it was represented at
an Army ceremonial parade at Bailleul in honour of the Duke of
Connaught, and three days later moved to its old camp   at

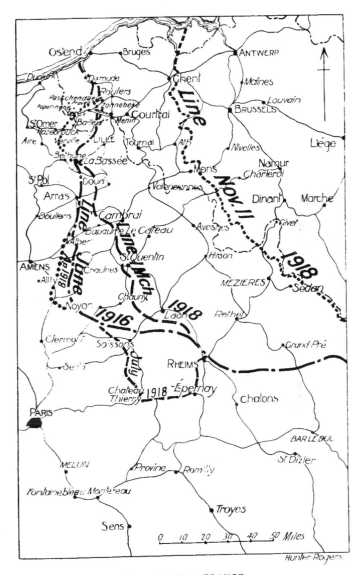

NORTHERN FRANCE.

Kortypyp and on the 30th to Hyde Park Corner, a well-known spot in Ploegsteert Wood in Belgium, just over the French frontier. Here the troops were accommodated in tunnels in Hill 63, known as the Catacombs, which were lit by electricity and provided with tiers of bunks, accommodating hundreds of men. These tunnels were very damp and the water had to be continually pumped out. As Hyde Park Corner was often bombarded with gas-shells, the entrances to the tunnels were protected by gas-proof doors. Whilst here the battalion was used for working and carrying parties, except those men who were at Kortypyp attending a battalion school for the training of n.c.o.'s, Lewis gunners, signallers and bombers.

For their fine work at Messines, the following honours were awarded to members of the battalions: D.S.O. 1; M.C. 4; D.C.M. 4; and M.M. 20. About this time, the division suffered a great loss by the death of the Divisional Commander, Major-General Holmes, who was killed at Ploegsteert Wood when making an inspection of the front in company of Mr. W. A. Holman, the then Premier of N.S.W. It was at Ploegsteert, too, that Major Howden (M.C. and Bar), an officer highly esteemed by the whole battalion, was killed. After his splendid work at Stormy Trench, Gueudecourt, he had been sent to the Senior Officers' School Aldershot, where he was strongly recommended to be a battalion commander. On his return he was transferred to the 48th Bn. as second-in-command, but on July 5th, at Ploegsteert, during breakfast, the officers' mess was shelled and this splendid young officer was killed. His promotion had been very rapid as he had been a private on Gallipoli in August 1915, but by his outstanding ability he had risen to Major and Second-in Command of a battalion in June 1917.

On July 18th the 45th was relieved and marched back to billets at Doullieu, where the usual cleaning up process was carried out. On July 27th General Plumer inspected it at a brigade parade, and the battalion, which was gradually increasing in strength, looked well. On August 6th, it was on the move again, marching to the Kemmel area and, next day, to Lumm Farm where it relieved the 13th Bn. of the Rifle Brigade in a reserve position. For the next week, it was engaged in digging the reserve line and in carrying supplies to the front line.

On the night of August 14th the 45th relieved the 48th Bn. in the front line east of Wambeke where the country was low-lying and wet, and the firing line was merely a series of posts connected by a shallow trench. Two companies were in the front line, the other two in support, and Battalion H.Q. at Cabin Hill. On the morning of August 14th and again on August 17th, enemy raiding parties were driven off by Lewis gun fire. The 45th sent out a patrol and secured identifications of the enemy battalion opposite. These identifications of enemy units were always valued by the Intelligence Staff at Army Headquarters as it enabled them to trace the movements of German divisions and forecast the enemy's probable intentions. In this sector the 45th had 5 other ranks killed and 32 other ranks wounded.

On the night of August 22nd, the battalion was relieved by the 2nd Bn. of the Wiltshire Regt., and next day marched to a camp near Dranoutre. It was inspected at its training by the Commander of the 2nd Anzac Corps and the new Divisional Commander, Major-General Sinclair-Maclagan. The latter was a Regular Officer of the British Army who had been Director of Drill at Duntroon at the outbreak of war, and had left Australia as the Commander of the 3rd Infantry Brigade. On August 28th the battalion moved to La Motte in the Forest of Nieppe and the next day, during a very heavy rainstorm, marched to Wallon-Cappel, near Staple. At this place large numbers of reinforcements were absorbed and it was anticipated that the brigade would shortly be going into action. Special attention was paid to the training of platoons in the offensive, as the platoon was the tactical unit. Whilst here the 45th was inspected by General Birdwood to whose Corps the division had reverted, and some men were presented with Military Medals.

On September 3rd the battalion moved by bus to Cuhem in the Bomy area, S.W. of Aire. The billets were not good but, though it was the first time Australians had been billeted in this locality, the diggers soon made friends with the hospitable French people. Vigorous training, including tactical exercises, was carried out and, in addition, battalion and brigade sports were held. On September 19th the 45th moved by busses to the Le Nieppe area where it was billeted at Maison Blanche, one of the biggest and most prosperous farms that the men had seen in France. Three days later it marched to Steenvoorde and its short rest was over. The 1st and 2nd Divisions had already been in action at the Menin Road and the 4th Division's turn had come to take part in the famous Passchendaele offensive.

CHAPTER XI.

PASSCHENDAELE.

On September 23rd the battalion moved by bus from Steenvoorde to Dominion Camp, S.E. of Poperinghe, and next day marched to Belgian Chateau, S.W. of Ypres. On the following day, it marched forward under Major Allen, to Westhoek Ridge, where the 12th Infantry Brigade was in divisional reserve for the big attack often known as the Battle cf Polygon Wood, carried out by the 4th and 5th Divisions on September 26th. Here, the 45th provided working parties for the repairing of the Westhoek-Zonnebeke road.

The day following this attack, the battalion moved forward and relieved the 50th in support on Anzac Ridge. On the night of Septmber 28th, it took over the right sub-sector of the divisional front from the 13th and 15th Bns. Four strong posts were established in front of the newly-captured line; vigorous patrolling was carried out, and a considerable amount of work was done in consolidating the position. Fierce fighting had been going on over the whole sector for the last six weeks; consequently the landscape was a scene of absolute desolation. Buildings were completely ruined, trees were gaunt spectres of their former state, guns and vehicles were derelict, and ammunition and engineering material were scattered about on all sides.

From "Belgian Chateau" forward, the route was through Ypres which, by this time, was in absolute ruins. Only a few broken walls were left of the once beautiful Cloth Hall and the Cathedral. The way out of Ypres was through the Menin Gate, and then one proceeded up the Menin Road, past Hell-Fire Corner, until Birr Cross Roads were reached. From here, the route went along a corduroy road, past Bellevarde Lake to Bellevarde Ridge. From this ridge, a track had been hastily constructed by Pioneer Battalions, leading to Westhoek Ridge. This track was a veritable death-trap as the German gunners knew its range to a yard. It was just wide enough for two waggons to pass, and, as the ground on either side had been literally ploughed up by shells, movement away from the plank road was impossible. The sights along it were both ghastly and pitiable. Every few yards dead horses or mules and broken vehicles could be seen, and the unburied bodies of dead men was no uncommon sight. The road was constantly packed with every sort of vehicular and pedestrian traffic which was repeatedly blocked by casualties from enemy shell-fire. The dead animals and shattered vehicles would be hurriedly tipped into adjacent shell holes and the dead and wounded men as quickly as possible evacuated to the rear. The long line of traffic would commence to move again slowly.

The feeding of the troops under conditions such as this was most difficult and yet, to the eternal credit of the commissariat of the whole British Army from the Quarter-Master-General down to the company cooks, the troops in the line were always rationed and, considering the circumstances, fed well.

On the night of September 30th, the battalion was relieved by the 2nd and went back to China Wall, just south of Hell-Fire Corner. During the period mentioned above, 17 other ranks were killed and 2 officers and 50 other ranks were wounded and Lieut. McLean was reported missing but believed killed. On October 1st, the battalion marched to Halifax Camp where the troops had an opportunity of using the divisional hot baths.

Two days later, it moved by bus to Steenvoorde where it was rejoined by the nucleus which had been left behind at the reinforcement camp at Caestre. About this time, Lieut.-Colonel Herring left to command No. 4 Divisional Group at Hurdcott, England. He had had a very long period of continuous active service and, whilst everybody was very sorry that he should leave the battalion, they were glad for his sake that he was to have a well-deserved rest. He had commanded the 45th with conspicuous success from its formation 20 months before, and the welfare of his men was always his first consideration. About the same time, Major Salier, the popular Brigade Major, left the Brigade to take up an important appointment with the Tank Corps, in England. His successor was Major E. A. Wilton, a Duntroon graduate who had commanded the 4th Machine Gun Company.

On October 9th, the battalion under the command of Major H. C Ford, who had been appointed temporarily, moved forward to Ypres. Major Ford had been with the 13th Bn. on Gallipoli, and had recently been second-in-command of the 46th. The 2nd Division had just made two heavy attacks at Broodseinde and, owing to its heavy casualties, the 45th Bn. was hurried forward that evening to relieve the 5th Infantry Brigade. The exact position of the front line was unknown, and the battalion had a very difficult task in taking over without being aware of the dispositions. In addition, the battalion had made a forced march from Ypres to Broodseinde Ridge. It completed the relief in the early hours of October 10th, having suffered 20 casualties. The position which was just south of the Ypres-Roulers railway line, was found to be a series of shell holes. Two companies were in the front line, two in support, and Bn. HQ. in a "pill-box" north of Broodseinde. Active patrolling was carried out, and in one patrol under Lieut. Watts all the members were wounded but managed to get back to our lines. Three prisoners were captured by a patrol under Sgt. Payne and another patrol under Cpl. George captured two Germans and killed another.

On October 11th the enemy's artillery was very active. Major Ford was wounded and Captain Dibbs took command until midnight when Major Allen arrived. At 4 a.m. on the 12th the 47th. and 48th Bns. made an attack in conjunction with the 3rd Division. The 45th Bn. co-operated by providing a party of 100 men under Capt. Adams to dig a communication trench to the first objective and two parties of 50 men each, under Lieuts. McNiven and Sorrell, established forward dumps for this attack. On October 13th the battalion was relieved and moved back to Esplanade Sap at Ypres. Here Major S. L. Perry, M.C. assumed command. During the three days at Broodseinde the 45th had 1 officer and 48 other ranks killed and 7 officers and 139 other ranks wounded.

On October 19th, the battalion went forward again and during a particularly heavy enemy bombardment relieved the 52nd Bn. in the right sub-sector of the divisional front. One company was in the front line, one in support and two in local reserve. Bn. HQ. was just south of Broodseinde. Throughout the last three months there had been phenomenal rains and during a great part of October it rained every day. The result was that the whole forward area was a quagmire. Traffic was restricted to the few narrow roads, and the infantry could not move away from the duck-boarded tracks on account of the mud. On October 20th, the 45th was relieved by the 13th and 16th Bns. and moved back to a bivouac site S.W. of Ypres. During this period at Broodseinde, 1 officer and 6 other ranks were killed and 9 other ranks were wounded. Amongst those killed was the Sergeant Cook, Sgt. Curtis, a great worker who had been indefatigable in his efforts to provide hot meals for the troops.

The work of the Transport Section and Quarter Master's staff in the Passchendaele area was splendid. The untiring example of the Transport Officer, Lieut. Fitzhardinge and the Transport Sergeant, Sgt. Robinson, the Q.M. Lieut. Neaves and

R.Q.M.S. McKinley, had been followed by all the members of their sections in the face of tremendous difficulties, three men of Q.M.'s staff being killed.

The Passchendaele offensive, which had been waged almost uninterruptedly for three months concluded with the capture by the Canadians of the highest part of Passchendaele Ridge. Further attacks were rendered impossible by the bad weather conditions, the almost impassable mud and the temporary exhaustion of the attacking troops. These offensives with limited objectives had of late generally been successful, but the enemy was usually able to withdraw his artillery and so to meet the next attack. The Germans made great use of concrete "pill-boxes" in defence, and the machine gun fire from these strong points was very destructive. Also the enemy's aeroplanes were very active, especially his bombing machines which caused many casualties amongst the troops and animals. Though the British Army suffered enormous casualties at Passchendaele this offensive achieved one of its main objects in relieving the pressure on the French Army, which had received a serious set-back in the previous April on the Chemin-des-Dames.

During the Passchendaele offensive, the battalion suffered the following casualties:—Lieutenants A. R. Muir, J. Kirman, J. McLean, and R. Lagden, and 70 other ranks were killed, and 8 officers and 210 other ranks were wounded.

On October 22nd the battalion marched back to Halifax Camp south of Vlamertinghe, where the nucleus rejoined it. On arrival in the back area, the first necessity was to obtain hot baths and clean clothing at the divisional baths, and so get rid of the mud accumulated on the slopes of Passchendaele. Four days later, the battalion entrained at Brandhoek and proceeded to Wizernes whence it was taken by buses to Erny St. Julien in the rest area. The 45th was now looking forward to a long spell out of the line as the whole division had not had a rest since the battalion was at Bresle six months before.

CHAPTER XII.

THE WINTER OF 1917-1918.

The 45th arrived at Erny St. Julien on October 26th and remained there for three weeks. A considerable amount of reorganisation had to be done as the result of the strenuous time at Passchendaele; and training, especially that of n.c.o's and specialists was resumed. Whilst at this place, Brigadier-General Robertson proceeded on six months leave to Australia, and Brigadier-General J. Gellibrand was appointed Brigade Commander. He was a Tasmanian who had resigned from the British Regular Army before the war, but had left Australia with the 1st Division.

At last it had been decided that the 4th Division should have a long rest in the back area south of Abbeville. This locality was 70 miles away from the billeting area then occupied, and the move was to be carried out by march route. On November 15th the journey began. The first day the battalion marched to Ruisseauville and the next day to Warbecourt. The third stage was to Toute-Fontaine and on the fourth day Fontaine-sur-Maye was reached. Whilst at this place some of the troops took the opportunity of visiting the battlefield of Crecy where Edward, the Black Prince, won his spurs in 1346. On November 20th the battalion marched to Hautvilliers and, next day, to Franleu. St. Quentin-la-Motte was reached on November 22nd. Here the troops expected to remain until at least after Christmas and at once began to make itself as comfortable as circumstances would permit. St. Quentin-la-Motte is a small village, two miles from the English Channel and five miles from Le Treport, a favourite seaside resort of English and Parisian tourists. The billets were good, and though it was winter the battalion spent a pleasant time there.

The afternoons were devoted to sport, and in the mornings training was carried out. The specialists attended battalion, brigade or divisional classes, and march discipline was maintained by frequent route-marches, through picturesque country. The training was, as usual, closely supervised by the Brigade Staff on which Major R. H. Norman was now the Brigade Major.

The stay at St. Quentin-la-Motte, however, was suddenly cut short by the order that the 4th Division should move at once to Peronne. At Cambrai, a big British attack, in which large numbers of tanks and cavalry had been used was at first wonderfully successful, but the Germans had launched a huge counter-offensive at the same place. The British Army was short of reserves owing to the casualties at Passchendaele and to the fact that several divisions had been sent to Italy, so the 4th Division was hurried down to this new scene of fighting as a reserve. On December 5th the battalion marched to Eu and entrained for Peronne, which was reached next day; and from there it went to a camp of tents at Haut Allaines. As it was expected that the brigade would have to go into action, numerous battalion and brigade tactical exercises were carried out.

On November 11th, the second referendum on conscription in Australia was held. In this referendum (which again negatived the proposal), very little interest was taken by the majority of the troops, who by this time were fatalists. Christmas Day, on which the snow lay thick around the tents, was observed as a holiday but, owing to the uncertainty of the battalion's movements no special preparations could be made to celebrate it. This month at Peronne was a miserable one, due to the poor accommodation and the severe cold. The battalion was constantly on the alert, as the 4th Division was the only reserve in this part of the line.

About this time Major Perry was promoted to Lieut.-Colonel and appointed to command the battalion. Capt. Varley was appointed Staff Captain of the 12th Infantry Brigade, and Lieut. R. S. Pickup succeeded him as Adjutant. Whilst at Haut-Allaines, congratulatory cards were presented by the Divisional Commander to 5 officers and 13 other ranks for their fine work at Passchendaele.

The crisis at Cambrai was now over and on January 8th during a heavy snow storm the battalion entrained at Peronne and once more moved north. Bailleul was reached the next day and the battalion marched to Meteren. It remained here only a few days as the brigade was to take over the front line in the Hollebeke sector. The battalion entrained at Godevaersvelde for St. Eloi and then marched to Spoilbank where it was accommodated in dugouts and a tunnel.

On January 11th, the battalion relieved the 13th Bn. of the Royal Fusiliers at Hollebeke, where the four battalions of the brigade were in the front line. One company was in the front line of posts, one in support, and two in local reserve. The weather was extremely cold; snow was thick on the ground and, after a thaw had set in, the mud and slush made the front line trenches very uncomfortable. To alleviate the hardships of the men in the front line, inter-company reliefs were carried out every second day and two hot meals were sent up to the men daily. The enemy's shelling was below normal in this sector, but during the nine days in the line, 1 other rank was killed and 20 other ranks wounded. Whilst here, Lieut. Sorrell and Sergeant McKane were selected for special service and, under secret orders, left for a destination unknown. They eventually reached Persia and Mesopotamia as members of the famous Dunsterville Force, whose exploits are so well known. About this time, Capt. Whiting was appointed Regimental Medical

Officer in place of Capt. S. Parker who had done such sterling work with the battalion.

On January 20th, the 45th was relieved by the 15th Bn. and marched back to Spoilbank. There it entrained for La Clytte and was accommodated at De Zon Camp. It was here that the battalion had its long delayed special Christmas dinner which was followed by a very enjoyable concert. The battalion worked very hard at constructing a Corps reserve line in this area. It was fully realised by General Headquarters that the Germans were concentrating on the western front the divisions that had been released from the eastern front after the signing of peace with the Russians; and as it was anticipated that the enemy would launch his big offensive shortly it was obviously essential to have strong reserve lines of defence in the northern sector, where the front line was so close to the Channel Ports.

The battalion moved forward to the front line again and on February 5th, relieved the 14th. Portion of the line had been held by the 45th previously, but this time two companies were in the front line, one in support, and one in reserve. Inter-company reliefs were carried out every four days and a lot of work was done to make the defence of this locality reasonably secure. Strong patrols examined the enemy's defences each night, and in this work the following officers and n.c.o.'s showed great initiative: Lieutenants T. W. Perry, McKay, Watts, Hughes and Frosts and Sergeants Lovett Bull and Kelly and Lance-Corporal Loolong. During this tour in the line, Lieut. A. Stevens was killed and 5 other ranks were wounded, whilst several men were affected by gas during a severe gas-shell bombardment by the enemy.

On February 13th the 45th was relieved by the 46 Bn. and moved back to Spoilbank whence it proceeded by motor lorry to Parrett Camp between Vierstraat and Kemmel. Whilst here it went through the usual cleaning up process and each day half the battalion was employed in constructing a reserve line, wiring the support line, burying telephone cable, or salvaging. On February 17th it marched back to billets at Meteren. Here the mornings were devoted to training, but in the afternoons there were organised sports. With plenty of sound training and healthy recreation, the morale of the troops became very high. The time for the long expected German offensive was fast approaching and the force was quite ready to meet it. Orders were received to be ready to move at very short notice and all surplus baggage was dumped at the school at Meteren.

At last the German blow fell. On March 21st the enemy launched a colossal attack on the 3rd and 5th British Armies from Arras to St. Quentin. Four days later the battalion left for the south to take its share in stopping the German advance.

CHAPTER XIII.

THE GERMAN ATTACK AT DERNANCOURT IN APRIL, 1918.

On March 21st, Ludendorff launched his long expected offensive on the right of the British line from Arras to the junction of the British and French Armies near St. Quentin. On the left the Third British Army repulsed the Germans with terrific losses or else gave ground slowly; but on the right, the front of the Fifth British Army was broken by the force of this smashing blow. In this sector the line had only a few months previously been taken over by the British from the French and the reserve lines were not nearly finished. Also the front of the Fifth British Army was very thinly held, owing to the lack of reserve divisions. The Germans attacked the British with more than three times the number of the formations that were holding this front. The object of this powerful offensive was to separate the British and French Armies and then attack them in turn when they would be unable to render each other mutual assistance.

Since January 1st, 1918, the five Australian Divisions had for the first time been united in one corps known as the Australian Army Corps. The First and Second Anzac Corps had ceased to exist.   At the opening of the German offensive in March, the Australian Corps was holding the front from Armentieres to Ypres, the 4th Division being in reserve in the Meteren area.

As the news of the unprecedented fighting down south came through, the 4th Division, which had already taken part in more battles in France than any of the other Australian divisions, knew that it was to be one of the first to be sent south. It was now a race against time to get to the scene of the fighting. At 10 a.m. on March 25th, the 45th Bn. embussed at Meteren for the Somme battlefield. It travelled all day passing en route through St. Pol, until it came to Bailleulmont on the main Arras-Doullens road which was reached at midnight.   This hurried move to the south by motor bus was full of interest.   Every road leading in a southerly direction was absolutely thick with traffic, and dense clouds of dust caused by the immense amount of mechanical and horse transport could be seen for miles. As the battalion approached the fighting zone, hundreds of French civilians fleeing before the German advance were seen. These refugees had pressed into service all kinds of transport to carry their goods and chattels. The streets in the towns and villages passed through were very congested, and the confusion was added to by numerous rumours regarding some fresh German victory or Allied counter-attack.

On the night of March 25th the battalion billeted at Bailleul-mont, and got some rest, but it was under orders to turn out at any moment. During the night piquets were posted on the outskirts of the village because the situation was very obscure. At 10 a.m. the next day, information was received that the enemy had broken through in armoured cars. This was afterwards found to be incorrect, but picquets were posted on the main roads outside the village and the officers reconnoitred the ridge between Berle-au-Bois and Bellacourt preparatory to the battalion taking up a defensive position. Shortly after midday the piquets were recalled, and, after the packs and surplus stores had been dumped, the 45th moved out for Hennescamp as the advance guard for the Brigade. When it had reached Berle-au-Bois, this move was cancelled, and the battalion marched back to Bailleulmont.

The regimental transport which had moved south by road, had rejoined the unit at midday. During its absence the task of obtaining rations was a difficult one for the Q.M. who, however, managed to commandeer a motor lorry for this purpose. On arrival of the transport, the troops were given a hot meal and the mobile reserve of ammunition was issued to the men who eagerly asked for as much of it as they could carry.

That night the 45th suddenly received orders to move and, at 10 p.m., it marched off in fighting order. All that night it marched, stopping only for a halt of ten minutes each hour and an occasional longer rest. At 7 a.m. the next morning it reached Senlis having covered a distance of 17 miles. This march through the night was a memorable one, as the route was only a few kilometres from the fluctuating line, and, owing to the presence of the enemy, it was necessary to have advanced and flank guards for the protection of the main body. The roads to the rear were congested with French civilians, the great majority of whom were walking and pushing handcarts or wheel barrows on which were piled their cherished belongings; others were leading or driving a few goats or cows. It was a pitiful sight to see old men, women, and children, plodding wearily along, leaving behind them their homes which soon would be in ruins.

On the morning of March 27th before the battalion had finished breakfast, it was ordered forward to the brigade concentration area near Millencourt. Though the situation was not clear, it was evident that the enemy had that morning captured Albert. The 47th and 48th Battalions immediately went into the line and relieved detachments of regiments of the 9th British division. The 45th took up a position of readiness N.E. of Millencourt and began to dig a support line. The brigade front extended along the railway embankment from Dernacourt to Albert.

Early on the morning of March 28th the enemy attacked the railway line, but was driven off leaving behind some prisoners, and during that day nine small attacks were made by him without success. At 1 a.m. that morning the 45th received orders to occupy a hill overlooking Dernancourt and to dig in before daylight. The battalion moved to this locality, marching on compass bearings and completed the digging of a defensive position before dawn. Owing to the heavy casualties suffered by the 47th the day before, "B" Company went forward and took over the front line near Dernancourt, and helped to repel the German attacks. Preparations were made by the remainder of the battalion to attack the village of Dernancourt, but this attack was cancelled. Throughout the evening numerous parties of Germans were observed moving up to the front line and his artillery became more active.

On the night of March 29th the battalion took over from the 47th the front line for a distance of half a mile north of Dernancourt, and was in touch with the 17th Bn. of the Lancashire Fusiliers on its right and the 48th Bn., A.I.F., on its left. Throughout the 30th and 31st March, it was engaged in strengthening the improvised front line. Dernancourt, which was only 300 yards distant and where the battalion had been so uncomfortably billeted in 1916, was held by the Germans. On April 1st, two Frenchwomen, who evidently had been unable to escape in time were seen in the village by our men. One of these women waved to our men to advance, and pointed behind her indicating that Germans were in her house. The diggers signalled back to her to come over to their post, but she made them understand that it was impossible.

The first three days in the line the battalion snipers were

busy and accounted for one German officer and twenty other ranks. At night patrols were sent out every hour to keep a watch on the movements of the enemy. On April 2nd twenty-five Germans were killed by the snipers. That night the battalion was relieved by the 47th Bn., and with the exception of "C" Company, which remained in reserve to the 47th, it moved back to the Lavieville-Ribemont line where it remained for two days. During the first nine days at Dernancourt, the battalion suffered the following casualties: Captain O. Dibbs, Lieut. Terras and 21 other ranks were killed, and 1 officer and 60 other ranks were wounded.

On the night of April 4th information was obtained from a captured German that the enemy intended to make a big attack at Dernancourt on the next day. The battalion accordingly moved forward to a support position about a mile N.W. of that village. En route to this position some casualties were suffered from heavy shelling, but under cover of a dense mist the battalion dug itself in. The enemy's barrage, consisting of H.E., shrapnel and gas shells, lasted for two and a half hours. At 9.30 a.m., it slackened and the enemy infantry attacked in great force, under the pressure of this big attack the battalions in the line were forced slowly back from the railway embankment, but at the same time heavy casualties were inflicted on the enemy. In this attack "C" Company which was in support to the 47th Bn. was ordered forward to reinforce the front line. Two platoons of this company, under Lieuts. Allen and McDiarmid, reinforced the front line, and the remainder, under the company commander Capt. Adams, moved forward and took up a strong defensive position which blocked the German advance in this sector. In this attack on "C" Company, Lance-Corporal Bannister, in order to get a better field of fire, placed his Lewis gun on the shoulder of Corporal Squires, and these two n.c.o.'s relieving one another alternately, kept on firing in full view of the enemy.

At 12 noon, the remainder of the 45th was ordered to move forward to the old support line which by this time had become our front line. At 2 p.m. orders were received that the battalion, in conjunction with the 49th Bn. on the right and the 47th Bn. on the left, was to make a counter-attack with the object of regaining the high ground west of Dernancourt. It was to have taken place at 2.30 p.m. but was postponed until 5.15 p.m. in order to allow the right battalion to get into position. This attack was made with "D" Company under Captain Davies on the right, "A" Company under Captain Holman on the left, "B" Company under Captain Ferguson in close support. 'C" Company was still attached to the 47th Bn., and took part in the attack with that battalion. This counter-stroke was made with great dash, the platoons and companies keeping excellent formation and maintaining touch with the units on the flanks. As they advanced, they suffered severely from the enemy's machine gun fire, but they kept steadily on until about a hundred yards from their objective when they charged with fixed bayonets. After some hand to hand fighting the enemy retreated in disorder, leaving behind prisoners and machine guns. The superior fighting qualities of the Australians had told, and the ridge was again in our possession. This counter attack was a notable one, as it was the first time the battalion had been engaged in open warfare; covering fire in some cases was given by the flanking platoons, and in other cases from Lewis guns fired from the hips as the Lewis gunners advanced.

In this action on April 5th, the battalion suffered and the following casualties:—Lieutenants Lindsay, T. W. Perry and McDiarmid, Second-Lieutenants A. K. McDonald, and A. K. Mitchell and 23 other ranks were killed; 7 officers and 73 other ranks were wounded; and 1 officer and 9 other ranks were missing.

This big attack by the Germans had been made by three divisions against only two Australian brigades, the 12th and the 13th. In spite of his overwhelming numerical superiority and the heavy artillery bombardment, the final gain by the enemy was only the railway embankment. If he had been allowed to retain the high ground west of Dernancourt, this tactical advantage might have had a serious effect on later operations in this sector. The superb defence and the spirited counter-attack by the two infantry brigades rendered abortive the enemy's efforts.

After it had successfully routed the enemy, the battalion took up an outpost position until it was relieved that night by the 46th. It then went back to the old support line from which it had advanced that afternoon. During April 6th, it remained in support, but had 3 other ranks killed and 20 other ranks wounded from enemy shell fire. That night it was relieved by the 22nd Bn. of the 2nd Division which had arrived from the north. The 45th then moved back to Baizieux for the night, and next day marched to Bussy-les-Daours. This was a long march, especially so soon after the recent heavy fightings, but not a man fell out. On reaching Bussy, the battalion band played the weary troops to their billets, and after a hot meal the men settled down to rest. Despite their weariness and heavy casualties, the morale of the troops was very high because they had helped to stop the previously victorious advance of the Germans. During the fortnight in the Dernancourt sector the battalion had the following casualties: Killed, 7 officers and 46 other ranks; wounded, 8 officers and 151 other ranks; missing, 1 officer and 40 other ranks, the majority of whom were later reported as killed; total casualties, 16 officers and 237 other ranks.

CHAPTER XIV.

SOUTH OF THE SOMME IN THE SUMMER OF 1918.

The few days at Bussy-les-Dauors were spent in getting ready for action again. The billets were comfortable and the Battalion Headquarters was located in a magnificent chateau which had been hurriedly vacated by the owners on the approach of the Germans. On April 10th, the battalion moved to Cardonette where the luxury of hot baths and clean clothing was indulged in. Here, Lieut.-Col. Perry rejoined the unit and took over the command from Major Allen who had commanded it at Dernancourt.

On April 12th, the 45th marched to Frechencourt where comfortable billets were again found, but next day it went to La Houssoye, a dirty, battered little village. Whilst here, the officers and n.c.o's reconnoitred the Corps reserve line from Franvillers to Heilly, which the battalion was to hold in the event of the enemy breaking through. At La Houssoye the unit lost the services of Major A. S. Allen, D.S.O., a very efficient and popular officer who was appointed second-in-command of the 48th Bn. which he also temporarily commanded.

On April 21st the 45th moved back to Querrieu, where for six days it remained in reserve in a state of readiness, under instructions to be ready to move at half an hour's notice. On April 27th, it relieved the 50th Bn. in the front line near Villiers Brettoneux, which had been recaptured in a magnificent counter-attack by the 13th and 15'th Infantry Brigades on April 25th. For the first time in its history the 45th was now fighting alongside French troops, having on its immediate right the 8th Zouave Regiment of the famous Moroccan Division. The battalion thus had the honour of holding the extreme right of the British line in France.

Very active patrolling was carried out by the front line companies in the vicinity of Monument Wood and a few prisoners were captured; also eight Germans were discovered in a cellar in Villiers Brettoneux where they had been since the attack on the 25th. On April 30th the battalion extended its right flank by taking over portion of the line from the French, and this line was advanced by the establishment of forward posts. On May 3rd, when the 48th Bn. attacked Monument Wood, "B" Company pushed forward its left flank to conform with the action of that battalion, to which it rendered valuable assistance in the attack.

On the night of May 4th, the 45th was relieved by the 51st and it then moved back to billets at Blangy-Trenville. Whilst here the battalion was informed that 1 D.C.M., 1 bar to the M.M., and 19 M.M.'s, had been awarded for the fighting at Dernancourt and that more honours were to follow. Two days later, it went forward and occupied a Corps reserve line known as the Blangy line and the Tronville Switch. The next night it went into support in the Cachy and Aubigny lines, with Battalion Headquarters at the Abbey in Bois l'Abbe. On the night of May 9th it went into support on the right flank in a position which was scarcely dug at all and which required a lot of work to convert into continuous line.

On May 14th the battalion relieved the 48th in the front line where it remained for eight days. Here Lieut.-Colonel Herring returned and took over command. Battalion Headquarters was situated at the chateau in Villiers-Brettoneux, which village at this time was not in absolute ruins, but, as time went on, became a total wreck. It had been a prosperous manufacturing town and much valuable material was salvaged and handed over to the French Mission which looked after the interests of the civilians in the war zone. Whilst in the line here, 13 other ranks were killed and 3 officers and 49 other ranks wounded. On the night of May 22nd, the right of the battalion front was taken over by the 44th, and the left by the 33rd Bn. The 45h then marched back to the Hospice St. Victor, at Rivery, near Amiens. Whilst here, it was notified that, in addition to the honours already announced for the fighting at Dernancourt, the following honours had been awarded: 1 D.S.O., 4 M.C.'s, 3 D.C.M.'s and 4 M.M.'s.

It was at Rivery, on May 25th, that 12 officers and 147 other ranks of the 47th Bn. were transferred to the 45th. Owing to the heavy casualties and the lack of sufficient reinforcements, the 47th had to be disbanded. The officers and other ranks of

Lieut.-Col. A. S. ALLEN,
D.S.O., C. de G. (France).

this splendid Queensland unit were split amongst the three remaining battalions of the 12th Infantry Brigade. It was a sad fate for so fine a corps as the 47th to lose its identity, but it had already happened to other Australian battalions for the same reasons. In fact before the Armistice, it was found necessary to disband one battalion in each brigade with the exception of the 1st, 2nd, 3rd and 4th Infantry Brigades. This left only 49 Infantry battalions, instead of 60 in the A.I.F. This reduction was the direct result of the two failures of conscription referendum, as sufficient volunteers were not coming forward to maintain the requisite number of infantry units in the five divisions. In order to ascertain which battalion of the brigade the officers and other ranks of the 47th Bn. wished to go to, a ballot was taken. It was a gratifying indication of the popularity of the 45th Bn. to find that 75 per cent. of the 47th voted for transfer to the 45th.

The battalion had a splendid time at Rivery. The Hospice St. Victor provided the most comfortable of billets and plenty of hot baths and clean clothing were available. Also the weather was fine and there were splendid opportunities for swimming in the neighbouring canal on which aquatic sports were held. The mornings were devoted to training, but the afternoons were free for sports and for visits in the neighbourhood. Rivery was on the River Somme which separated it from Amiens. This famous city which the Australians had saved from the Germans, is a very big one but, at this time, was almost deserted. It resembled a city of the dead, for there were thousands of empty houses and closed shops and not a living soul to be seen. It was frequently shelled and was bombed night and day, especially the railway station which was an important junction. Much damage was done to the buildings, and, even the Cathedral, a particularly fine edifice, though protected as much as possible, did not remain unscathed.

A short way up the river was Camon, and between this place and Rivery were some beautiful gardens. These gardens were on small islands in an area which had formerly been a swamp but had since been well drained by numerous canals. Cottages, overgrown with climbing roses, were built on these islands, which were connected by rustic bridges. It was summertime, so the gardens were looking their best; all kinds of flowers were in bloom, vegetables were growing to perfection, and there was ripe friut in the orchards. As these gardens were absolutely deserted, the troops naturally made themselves at home.

The battalion had already learnt from experience that these

pleasant times out of the line soon came to a sudden end, and in June it once more moved forward, and, less "D" and "C" Companies, relieved the 30th Bn. in a support position on the south side of the Somme near Daours. The other two companies occupied some support trenches half way between Villiers-Brettoneux and Corbie. During this period the 45th was engaged in training and in providing working parties for trench digging, salvaging, and burying telephone cable.

About this time many important changes took place in the command of formations and units in the Australian Corps. General Birdwood was given the command of the reconstructed Fifth British Army, and he took with him as his Chief Staff Officer, Major-General White, who had been so closely associated with the A.I.F. since its formation. General Birdwood, however, still retained his appointment of G.O.C. of the A.I.F. The command of the Australian Corps was given to Lieut.-General Monash, who had commanded the 4th Infantry Brigade on Gallipoli and the 3rd Division in France. Major-General Gellibrand was appointed to command the 3rd Division and he was succeeded in the command of the 12th Infantry Brigade by Brigadier-General Leane, who had been C.O. of the 48th Bn. When Lt.-Col. Herring returned from England in the early part of May, Lt.-Col. Perry was transferred to command the 48th Bn. and Major Allen rejoined the 45th Bn. Shortly afterwards, Lieut.Colonel Herring was promoted to be Brigadier-General and appointed to command the 13th Infantry Brigade, Major Allen assumed command for a few days and then was selected to attend a Senior Officers' Course in England, lasting several months. Lieut.-Colonel C. M. Johnston, D.S.O., from the 14th Bn., was then appointed to command the 45th.

On the night of June 16th, the battalion relieved the 50th Bn. in the front line near Vaire-sur-Corbie. "B" Company was on the right, "A" in the centre, "D" on the left, and "C" in support. During this relief, the last-named company suffered 11 casualties, including one killed, from enemy shell fire.

During the tour in the line here, several American officers and n.c.o.'s from the 33rd American Division were attached to the 45th for periods of four days. The outstanding features of these attachments of the Americans were their ignorance of modern warfare and their keenness to remedy that defect. They were very popular with the Australians and were reluctant to leave when their time was up. Americans were just beginning to arrive in France in very large numbers, and many of their officers and other ranks were attached for instruction to Australian units as well as to the British and the French.

Inter-company reliefs were carried out and this allowed the support company to obtain hot baths at Battalion Headquarters where improvised baths were erected. Cleanliness was an all important factor in keeping the troops fit, as it had been conclusively proved that the vermin, which infected the trenches, were one of the chief disseminators of disease.

On the night of June 30th a party of 7 n.c.o.'s and men under Lieut. Morton, went out to secure a prisoner in order to identify the German division in this part of the line. They ran across a party of 30 Germans whom the patrol rushed with revolvers and bombs, killing or wounding several of the enemy. Lieut. Morton and Private Patterson captured one German and brought him back to our lines.

During this period in the line, the enemy shelled Vaire with gas shells including the chateau in the bend of the river where Battalion Headquarters was situated. This chateau had been hurriedly vacated by the owner, who had left behind the furniture including a piano and a billiard table. A cow and a couple of goats which had also been abandoned, provided fresh milk, a welcome addition to the army ration.

On the night of July 2nd the battalion was relieved by the 42nd, which was to participate in the Battle of Hamel. On relief the 45th went into reserve in some trenches at La Neuville. The Battle of Hamel, the first big operation by the Australian Corps under the command of General Monash, was a great success. It was in this action that the 4th Division regained complete confidence in the Tanks, which played an important part in this battle. On the night of July 5th, the battalion relieved the 42nd in the newly-captured line from the north of Hamel to the Somme Canal, near Bouzencourt. Two nights later, in conjunction with an attack made by the 46th Bn. north of the Somme, it advanced its line. This minor operation was carried out by "C" and "D" Companies under the command of Captain Adams, D.S.O., M.C. These companies went forward and dug a new line of posts which gave a much better field of fire than those they had taken over. "B" Company supplied working parties for the erection of wire entanglements, and, whilst this was being done, the whole battalion front was protected by covering parties of rifle and Lewis gun sections. When the enemy discovered what was in progress, he retaliated with a fierce bombardment, using gas shells. Our casualties were 7 other ranks wounded, 6 other ranks gassed, and Sgt. Montgomery, who had left Australia with the original 13th Bn., killed. The total casualties suffered in the line at Hamel were 3 other ranks killed and 40 wounded, including those gassed.

On the night of July 12th, the 33rd Bn. took over the front line in one of the best carried out reliefs that the battalion had experienced. It stayed that night at La Neuville and the next day marched to Cardonnette, where the nucleus rejoined the unit. Here the usual cleaning-up process was gone through and the 45th soon began to look well again after its long period in the front line. At Cardonnette the officers mess was revived for the first time for eight months. Training was resumed, and on July 18th, the battalion marched to the rifle range at the Citadel at Amiens and carried out musketry practices. Two days later it took part in a practice attack with Tanks at Vaux-en-Amienois. These Tanks were a great improvement on those with which the 45th had operated in the previous year, at Messines. From these preparations it was concluded that a big offensive was brewing on the British front.

On July 22nd, the 4th Division held a most successful race meeting at Allonville. Thousands of soldier spectators, mostly Australians, but including English, Scotch, Irish, New Zealanders, Canadians, Americans, French, and Belgians were present. They came to this race meeting in motor cars, lorries and waggons, on horses and bicycles, by foot, and even in aeroplanes. It was an extraordinary spectacle seeing that it was held only nine miles from the firing line. No doubt the German observers reported that the "mad" British were indulging in sport again. In any case it probably served a useful purpose in allaying any suspicions caused by the recent activity in connection with the forthcoming offensive. Two days later, the 12th Infantry Brigade also held a successful race meeting and the next day the Battalion Sports culminated this series of festivities.

With the approach of the big offensive, the battalion once more got into fighting trim; kits and surplus stores were dumped, and the nucleus to be left behind was detailed. On July 31st the battalion began its approach march to the concentration area. It first went to Cagny, S.E. of Amiens, where it bivouacked in an orchard which concealed it from observation from the air. It remained here until August 2nd, and then went to St. Nicholas near Boves, where it took over bivouacs from a unit of a French Colonial Regiment.

The big offensive which was impending was so well stage-managed that very little information as to the exact location and date of the attack could be gathered by the rank and file.

The greatest secrecy prevailed, and all abnormal movement took place at night. At 9 p.m. on August 4th the battalion moved forward to a position west of Hamel. The night was dark and the roads so congested with traffic that the 45th did not reach its destination until 2 o'clock next morning. It remained here for three days and made all the final preparations for the big offensive which took place on August 8th, which Ludendorff afterwards called "the black day" for Germany.

CHAPTER XV.

THE GREAT VICTORY OF AUGUST 8th.

The great allied offensive east of Amiens on August 8th was made by the Fourth British Army in conjunction with the French on the right. The spearhead of the British attack was the Australian Corps, with the Canadian Corps, on its right and the Third British Corps on its left, north of the River Somme.

The Australian Corps had a frontage of 7000 yards, reaching from Villiers-Brettoneux to the Somme. On the first day the 2nd, 3rd, 4th and 5th Divisions were used in the attack and the 1st Division, which had just arrived from the Hazebrouck sector, was in reserve. The advance was to be made by the "leap-frog" method—i.e., one division passing through another and carrying on the attack. The first phase was to be carried out by the 2nd and 3rd Divisions, the former on the right, east of Villiers-Brettoneux, and the latter from the east of Hamel to the Somme. These two divisions advanced 3000 yards under cover of a heavy artillery barrage and with the aid of Tanks.

The second phase of the attack was to be carried out by the 5th and 4th divisions which were to "leap-frog" through the 2nd and 3rd Divisions respectively. These two divisions in the second phase were to advance 4500 yards under semi-open warfare conditions. The attack of the 4th Division would be delivered by the 4th and 12th Infantry Brigades, with the latter on the right. The divisional reserve was the 1st Infantry Brigade, temporarily replacing the 13th Infantry Brigade which had taken over the front line formerly held by the French between Villiers-Brettoneux and Hangaard Wood. The 13th Infantry Brigade held this portion of the line to conceal the concentration of the Canadian Corps which was to attack in that sector.

The first phase of the assault for which zero hour was 4.30 a.m. was a complete success. This attack which was made under a terrific barrage, aided by numerous Tanks and under cover of a dense fog, took the Germans completely by surprise. Thousands of prisoners and numerous guns were captured with comparatively small losses to our troops. During the first phase, those units of the 4th Division which were to attack in the second phase, moved forward from their concentration area to their positions of assembly.

At 4 a.m. the 45th Bn. was in its first position of assembly and at 5.30 a.m. it moved forward to the second position, in artillery formation with platoons in single file. "A" and "B" Companies were in front and were followed by the other companies with Battalion Headquarters and the pack animals in rear. Owing to the dense fog and the dust and smoke from the barrage, it was difficult to locate the second position of assembly but this was reached in good time by 7 a.m. Here the battalion was met by the Intelligence Officer and battalion scouts who had guided to this place the six Mark V Tanks which were to co-operate with the Bn.

At 8 a.m. the 45th passed the jumping-off line and advanced in artillery formation with the Tanks and scouts forming a screen in front. Half an hour later, or four hours after the first zero, the battalion crossed the so-called green line which was the objective reached by the most advanced troops of the 3rd Division that morning. The advance from here went like clockwork, "A" and "B" Companies going straight ahead, leaving the "mopping-up" of the woods and dug-outs to "C" and "D" Companies. The 45th was in direct touch with the 46th Bn. on the right and the 13th on the left.

The Germans were absolutely overwhelmed by the strength and suddenness of this second attack. Though occasional machine gun crews put up a stiff fight, the majority of the enemy either freely surrendered or retreated precipitately. The battalion's objective (or red line, as it was called) was gained at 10.20 a.m. The whole attack had been a magnificent success, one of the outstanding features being the splendid co-operation between the Tanks and the Infantry. The casualties of the battalion had been very light compared with those of other battles, in that 4 other ranks were killed and 44 other ranks wounded.

The captures by the 45th in this attack were enormous as in two hours it captured 400 prisoners and an immense amount of war material including the following enemy artillery most of which was undamaged:—Three 8-inch Howitzers, five 6-inch long range guns, five 5.9-inch Howitzers, five 4.2-inch Howitzers, seven 77 mm. field guns, eight 3-inch minenwerfers and eighteen machine guns. This huge haul of prisoners and guns must surely be a record for any battalion in one attack, especially when the small losses are also taken into account.

On the night of August 8th, the 45th took over the line captured by the 48th which had advanced through the 45th and 46th earlier in the day to exploit their success. This line extended from the main Warfus-ee-Abancourt road to the S.W. of Proyart. During the night, which passed quietly, a hot meal was served to the troops who were feeling the need of it after their strenuous day. On August 9th, a daylight patrol under Lieut. Potts penetrated into enemy territory for a distance of half a mile, and brought back valuable information. During the last two days there had been much aerial activity on both sides. An innovation which saved the carrying parties a considerable amount of work was the transporting of small arms ammunition by aeroplanes which dropped it in packets behind our front line. During the night, the front line was advanced in conjunction with the advance by the units on the flanks and August 10th was spent in consolidating this new line. That night the battalion was relieved by the 33rd during a very heavy enemy bombardment of gas shells. The 45th then went back to Sailly-Laurette just north of the Somme, where it remained for two days enjoying a good rest and the pleasure of bathing in the Somme Canal.

On the night of August 13th, the battalion moved forward to an old system of trenches S.E. of Harbonnieres. During this day, the enemy's aircraft was particularly busy in bombing the forward approaches. At Harbonnieres, preparations were made for another attack, but this was cancelled. The 4th Division had now begun to take over from the 1st Division on the right, and, on the night of August 15th, the 45th battalion relieved the 3rd in the Lihons sector. This part of the line was portion of an old system of trenches that the French had occupied in 1916 prior to the First Battle of the Somme, and was now in a most dilapidated condition, being overgrown with weeds and bushes. These trenches formed an absolute maze, and the enemy's line was only 50 yards away, with numerous communication trenches between it and the Australian front.

This juxtaposition of the two trench systems near Lihons led to numerous encounters. On August 17th the enemy was very active, and several times crept along the communication trenches and attacked outposts with "stick" bombs, to which our men replied with the "Mills." On one occasion, Second-Lieutenant Lozelle and three other ranks gallantly rushed one troublesome post but unfortunately all the attackers were wounded. On August 19th, the battalion front was shelled very heavily by the enemy in retaliation for an attack carried out by the Canadians who were on the right. That night the 48th Bn. relieved the 45th which went back into reserve. Whilst in this reserve position, it was able to get hot baths and clean clothing at Harbonnieres. A considerable amount of salvage work as well as the digging and wiring of a reserve line was also done here.

On the night of August 24th, the battalion was relieved by two units of the 59th and 83rd French Regiments. During this relief, the enemy put down a very heavy gas shell barrage and the troops had to wear their gas masks for an hour, but owing to the good anti-gas discipline, the 45th did not suffer many casualties. After relief it marched to Harbonnieres where it embussed at 2 a.m. the next morning for Vaux-en-Amienois.

For nearly a fortnight the 45th remained at Vaux-en-Amienois in very comfortable billets. On September 7th, it marched out of the village to the stirring music of the band, and embussed for Biaches just west of Peronne. All that was left of Biaches was the name on a notice board; otherwise one would never have known that a village had been there. On September 9th, the battalion marched to Stable Wood near Cartigny and next day moved forward to bivouacs east of Estrees. The following night it again moved forward and took up a position near Poeilly. The stage was now set for yet another big attack by the 4th Division.

CHAPTER XVI.

LE VERGUIER, SEPTEMBER 18th.

The great Allied offensive had now been in progress for six weeks. The British, French and American Armies had successfully delivered attack after attack against the German Armies, the reason for this effort being that, after the sweeping victory on August 8th, Marshal Foch considered it very probable that a final victory could be obtained on the Western Front before the end of the year. All the British Armies were advancing victoriously, and the French and Americans were winning great victories as far south as the Argonne.

Lt.-Col. N. M. LOUTIT, D.S.O. and Bar.

After the victorious advance of the five Australian divisions from Villiers-Brettoneux to Lihons, the 1st Division had thrust with wonderful success at Chuignes.   Meanwhile, the 3rd Division had fought its way along the north bank of the Somme, the 2nd and 5th Divisions had subsequently forced the Germans across the Somme near Peronne, the 2nd Division having, in the first week of September, by a superb attack, stormed Mont St. Quentin, whilst the 5th Division captured Peronne and the 3rd Division seized the high ground at Bouchavesnes.   The German Army was now reeling backwards under this succession of rapid blows, and on September 18th, the Hindenburg Outpost Line was to be attacked, the 1st Division taking Hargicourt whilst the 4th Division went for Le Verguier.

On the night of September 16th, the 4th and 12th Infantry Brigades, relieved the 13th Infantry Brigade in the line west of Le Verguier.   The 12th was to attack on the right of the 4th, on whose left flank was the 1st Division.   As far as the 12th Brigade was concerned, the assault was to be made in three stages on a one battalion front of 1500 yards.   The 48th Bn. was to take the first objective, the 45th the second and the 46th the third.   Prior to the attack, the 45th was in support in a railway cutting S.E. of Vendelles where on September 17th, it made its final preparations for the attack on the morrow.

The battalion was astir early on the morning of September 18th; breakfast was at 3.30 a.m. and an hour later the 45th moved forward to its assembly position.   This approach was made in artillery formation with "A," "B" and "D" Companies in line in front, and "C" Company and Battalion Headquarters about 100 yards in rear.   As the unit moved up, rain fell steadily and, with the coming of dawn, there was a heavy fog.   At 5.20 a.m. our artillery barrage opened up, and a few minutes later, the battalion began to advance, keeping some 600 yards behind the 48th which was to take the first objective.

As the 45th crossed the forming up line, it was shelled heavily by the enemy and a number of casualties resulted.   A short halt was made near Cambrieres Wood, and after the 48th Bn. had very successfully gained its objective at 6.30 a.m., the 45th moved to a sunken road where it halted for half-an-hour whilst our artillery shelled the enemy's position.   It was now the turn of the 45th to attack in conjunction with a battalion of the Royal Sussex Regiment on its right, and the 13th Bn. A.I.F. on its left.

At 8.8 a.m. the 45th advanced through the 48th and proceeded to capture its objective, which was known as the red line.

The enemy was encountered in large numbers, but only in a few instances did he put up a stiff fight. The accuracy of our Lewis gun fire inflicted many casualties, and prisoners surrendered freely. The three front companies went straight ahead and left the "mopping up" to be done by "C" Company. The objective was gained at 9.20 a.m., and the battalion at once sent out strong patrols whilst it dug itself in. Later in the day, the 46th Bn. passed through this line and after capturing its objective, exploited the success that night.

In this battle in which both divisions completely succeeded, the 45th Bn. captured over 300 prisoners, two 5.9-inch Howitzers, three 77 mm. field guns and 15 machine guns. The battalion suffered the following casualties chiefly from artillery fire and from machine guns on the right flank: Lieutenants Horne, Hill and Hines, Second-Lieutenant Dietze and 6 other ranks were killed; Lieut.-Colonel Loutit, Captain Adams and 62 other ranks were wounded. Lieut.-Colonel N. M. Loutit, D.S.O., from the 50th Bn. had been appointed Commanding Officer of the battalion in the place of Lieut.-Colonel Johnston, who had been appointed C.O. of the 15th Bn.

During the next three days the 45th was engaged in consolidating the position gained, but on September 21st, it was relieved by the 5th Bn. of the Leicestershire Regt., and then marched back to Tincourt Wood. This attack on September 18th was a wonderful success as the attacking infantry of the 4th Division numbered only 3000 men, yet that division alone captured 2500 prisoners and many guns besides killing or wounding hundreds of Germans. The total casualties of the 4th Division were relatively small, numbering 500. In addition, the Hindenburg Outpost Line had been captured, with the result that our fire now swept the whole of the intervening ground down to the St. Quentin Canal, and thus paved the way for the breaking through of the redoubtable Hindenburg Line a fortnight later.

On September 23rd the 45th marched back to Assevillers, west of Peronne, where it occupied some huts and dug-outs. Here it was rejoined by the nucleus and the band. Meanwhile Lieut.-Colonel J. T. E. T. C. Ridley, D.S.O., from the 51st had been temporarily appointed C.O. On September 24th the battalion marched to Herbecourt where it embussed for Fluy, from which place it marched to Pissy in the rest area S.W. of Amiens.

The 1st and 4th Divisions were now out for a long rest. At the end of September, the 3rd and 5th Divisions captured the

Hindenburg Line in the vicinity of Bellicourt and, in the first week of October, the 2nd Division broke through the Beaurevoir Line and fought the last action in which Australian infantry were engaged—the capture of Montbrehain on October 12th. As events turned out, the Battle of Le Verguier on September 18th was the last fight of the 4th Division. Except for some of its officers and n.c.o.'s who were selected for liaison work with the 28th and 30th American Divisions, the division remained in the rest area S.W. of Amiens, until the cessation of hostilities. After the Battle of Montbrehain, the whole Australian Corps, with the exception of the artillery which assisted the advance of the British divisions, was out for a rest, and before it could be employed again the Germans capitulated.

At Pissy the battalion spent the period in training and in keeping the men fit by sport. In the first week of November, preparations were made for a move forward, but this move was postponed from day to day, and, on the morning of November 11th, the glad news of the Armistice came through.

CHAPTER XVII.

AFTER THE ARMISTICE IN BELGIUM, AND DEMOBILISATION.

The troops received the news of the Armistice with feelings of great relief but with a calmness that was remarkable considering what the cessation of hostilities really meant to them. They felt like one, who, awakened from a hideous nightmare, can scarcely believe that it is all over and he is still alive. However, the French civilians and the troops on leave in London and Paris, gave full vent to their pent-up feelings. In London, especially, the joy of the people who are considered unemotional, was as spontaneous and hilarious as it was indescribable.

On the day after the Armistice, the 45th left Pissy for Ailly-sur-Somme, where it entrained for Roisel which was reached on November 13th. The battalion remained here for one day and on the next, was transported by light railway to Brancourt-le-Grand, from which place it marched to Fresnoy-le-Grand.

By the terms of the Armistice, French, British, Belgian and American Armies were to occupy that part of Germany up to the Rhine and certain bridgeheads across this river. The British

Army of Occupation was to hold the bridgehead at Cologne. It was at first thought that two Australian Divisions would take part in this triumphal march to the Rhine, and the 4th Division probably would have been one of them. In order that the battalion should look its best in this fitting climax of its splendid career, special attention was paid to the furbishing of uniforms and equipment and to ceremonial drill. However, it was not to be. Orders were received from the Commonwealth Government that no Australian Division was to take part in the march into Germany. It was a great pity that the Australian Corps was not represented by at least one of its famous divisions in this last phase of the war.

As the Allied Armies followed the retreating enemy to the Rhine, the Australian Corps advanced into Belgium. On November 22nd, the battalion marched to St. Souplet and the next day to Favril. On November 26th it moved to Grand Fayt and the next day Avesnelles was reached. These marches were carried out under difficulties, for not only were the roads wet and muddy, but there was a constant stream of traffic moving towards Germany. On December 1st His Majesty the King drove through the brigade area, and the troops lined the roads to welcome him.

On December 13th the battalion under the command of Lieut.-Colonel Loutit, who had returned from hospital, marched to Sivry which is in Belgium just across the French frontier. The next day Boussu-lez-Waulcourt was reached, and on the following day St. Aubin. On December 16th, the 45th did its last trek as a complete unit when it marched to Hastiere-Levaux on the left bank of the Meuse, south of Dinant. It was most hospitably received by these Belgian civilians, who now saw Australian soldiers for the first time. In this part of Belgium, these people, who were Walloons or French-speaking Belgians, had been very badly treated by the Germans, especially in the early days of the war. A large part of this pretty little town had been destroyed, and the inhabitants had suffered cruel hardships.

Three days after the arrival at Hastiere-Levaux, the battalion was reviewed by H.R.H. the Prince of Wales. This inspection was its last formal parade as the process of demobilisation and repatriation of troops to Australia had now commenced.

The demobilisation and repatriation of the A.I.F. was an immense undertaking. The troops who had left Australia first were sent by drafts to England and thence to Australia as quickly as shipping could be provided. As each draft left the strength of the 45th decreased until the battalion became only a skeleton of its former self. Whilst awaiting demobilisation, very little training was done; only sufficient to keep the men fit and to maintain the standard of discipline. In order to prepare the men for their re-entry into civil life, a big system of educational training and non-military employment was inaugurated. A special Educational Corps was created and instructors were provided for all kinds of subjects. Classes were formed for instruction in subjects ranging from elementary arithmetic and English to those of a highly technical nature. Men, who in England were awaiting repatriation, were able to avail themselves of the opportunity to be attached to various colleges, industrial works and factories. The health of the troops was maintained by athletic competitions and sports.

Before the 45th left Hastiere-Levaux, portion of the mobilisation equipment, including the technical stores and ammunition, was handed back to Ordnance. On February 22nd, 1919, what was left of the battalion moved to Florennes. The men, though they were anxious to get back to Australia, were sorry to leave Hastiere-Levaux for another village as they had become very popular with the local inhabitants. The following letter sent to the C.O. of the battalion by the Burgomaster of Hastiere-Levaux speaks for itself :—

"The Australian troops left our locality some days ago and I beg you to accept the liveliest feelings of sympathy from the population, which will always keep a good remembrance of the 45th Bn. We admire the Australians for their generous patriotism which voluntarily brought them to our battlefields. We love them for their sufferings, and we send them our deepest gratitude for the active part they took in our deliverance. We received and welcomed you according to our small means, and we wanted our village to be hospitably agreeable, so that after those anxious years you might enjoy a happy and quiet life. We are proud that we were designed to receive you, and you may be sure that these two months you stayed here have tightened the bonds of friendship and gratitude which attach us to the brave sons of beautiful Australia. To all we wish a happy return to their far-away country."

With the gradual demobilisation of the Australian Corps it was necessary to concentrate the depleted units so the battalion stopped one night only at Florennes, and the next morning marched to Thy-le-Chateau. Here the Lewis guns were handed back to Ordnance, and about the middle of March the horses and mules were sold, many of them bringing high prices. The strength of the battalion was a fast diminishing quantity and, on March 24th, the attenuated 45th moved to Nalinnes, where the three battalions of the brigade were billeted. On April 4th a move was made to Acoz, and here arrangements were made for the final handing over of regimental records and stores. On April 14th a still closer concentration of the troops was made and the battalion moved to Bouffioulx. This move was the last until the final one to the Base. At Bouffioulx the last of the mobilisation stores and the regimental records were satisfactorily handed back.

On May 2nd, 1919, the last draft from the 45th Bn. moved to Charleroi and then entrained for the Base. From here it went to England and thence to Australia. After a glorious life of three years and two months on active service in Egypt, France and Belgium, the 45th Battalion had ceased to exist as a unit, but it will always be proudly remembered by the members who survived and by the next-of-kin of the gallant dead.

The memory of the 45th Bn. A.I.F. has been perpetuated by the formation of the 45th Bn. A.M.F. The Headquarters of this unit are at Kogarah, Sydney, and its members are drawn from the trainees who live in the suburbs of Kogarah, Arncliffe and Hurstville. The Citizen Force battalion has been given the honour of carrying the King's Colour and of emblazoning on its Regimental Colour the Battle Honours of the 45th Bn. A.I.F. May the memory of the sacrifices and heroic deeds of the overseas battalion be ever an inspiration to the home unit, and may the latter always uphold the honour of Australia as gloriously as did the 45th in the World War of 1914-1919.

"Dulce et decorum est pro patria mori."

APPENDIX I.

STATISTICS RELATING TO THE 45th Bn., A.I.F.

(1) NUMBER OF ALL RANKS WHOSE NAMES APPEAR ON THE NOMINAL ROLL:—

Officers	155
Other Ranks	3502
Medical Officers attached	4
Chaplains attached	4
Total	3665 all ranks

The above figures are taken from the official Nominal Roll (vide appendix 11) supplied by Base Records, Melbourne. They include officers and other ranks who were seconded to other units and those who were at one time on the strength of the battalion, but afterwards transferred to other units.

(2) CASUALTIES:—

	Officers	Other ranks
Killed in Action	33 ..	477
Died of Wounds	3 ..	147
Died of Disease	— ..	23
Died of Gas Poisoning ..	— ..	1
Died from other causes ..	— ..	10
Total	36 ..	654
Wounded in action	51 ..	1608
Gassed	— ..	48
Prisoners of War	2 ..	29
Total Battle Casualties ..	89 ..	2339

The above figures are taken from the Statistics of Casualties compiled by the Records Section, A.I.F. Headquarters, London, 30th June, 1919. They do not include casualties suffered by members when seconded to other units nor any wounds received by members when with other units prior to joining or after being transferred from the battalion.

(3) HONOURS AND DECORATIONS:—

The most Distinguished Order of St. Michael and St. George. (C.M.G.)	1
The Distinguished Service Order (D.S.O.)	4
Military Cross (M.C.)	30
Bar the Military Cross	5
Distinguished Conduct Medal (D.C.M.)	32
Military Medal (M.M.)	134

Bar to the Military Medal   1
Second Bar to the Military Medal   1
Meritorious Service Medal (M.S.M.)   3
Legion d'honneur Croix d'Officer   1
Croix de Guerre (French)   2
Croix de Guerre (Belgian)   1
Serbian Gold Medal   1
Mentions in Despatches   21

The above honours and decorations are those shown in the Official Description of Deeds in Action for which awards were made (vide Appendix 111, provided by Base Records, Melbourne). They do not include any honours or decorations awarded to members when with other units, prior to joining or after being transferred from the battalion.

(4) PRISONERS OF WAR AND WAR MATERIAL CAP-
      TURED BY THE BATTALION:—

German Prisoners of War   950
German Guns and Howitzers   30
German Trench Mortars   10
German Machine Guns   40

The above figures are compiled from the Battalion Monthly War Diary.

(5) NUMBER OF MOVES MADE BY THE BATTALION:—

Formation of the Battalion at Tel-el-Kebir, Egypt   2/3/16
Arrival in France 8/6/16
Last move of the complete Battalion to Hastiere-
      Levaux, Belgium 16/12/18
Last Draft from the Battalion for demobilisation
      left Charleroi, Belgium 2/5/19

During the period of two years and ten months from the formation until the last movement of the complete battalion, it made 188 moves from one locality to another averaging one in every five days. These movements were those of the whole battalion, which stayed at least one night in each place. Of course, the companies made many others in consequence of the frequent inter-company reliefs when in the line. This information was compiled from the Battalion Monthly War Diary.

APPENDIX II.

OFFICIAL DESCRIPTION OF THE BATTLE DEEDS FOR WHICH HONOURS WERE AWARDED.

Captain ADAMS, William George, D.S.O., M.C. (M.I.D.)

D.S.O.—For his excellent leadership, courage and devotion to duty during the enemy attack near DERNANCOURT, South, South West of ALBERT on April 5th, 1918.

When the Battn. was moving up to support a Battn. in the front line a heavy barrage fell. The Battn. was ordered to dig in, and it was due to the splendid organisation and coolness and skill in picking up a site for his company, coupled with the control of his men, that many casualties were averted. He then moved forward through the barrage and took charge of another company which was well forward, and found that this company was being surrounded by the enemy. He extricated them with great skill and occupied a position a little further back which he held for two hours against very heavy odds, inflicting heavy casualities. After the Reserve line had been properly manned he withdrew to this 'ne. In the attack on the afternoon of 5th April, 1918, he was the chief means of getting information back to the troops in the attack and Battn. H.Q., going up many times personally to see what was being done and keeping H.Q. informed all through the attack and subsequent consolidation of the position taken. His work during the whole tour showed a splendid example of skill, courage and sound judgment which inspired all ranks with absolute confidence, and was a great factor in the success of the tour.

Captain ADAMS, William George, D.S.O., M.C. (M.I.D.)

M.C.—For great courage and leadership, whilst in command of his Company at ZONNEBEKE on 12th October, 1917. He went forward and made personal reconnaissance, the result of which kept his Battn. Commander in close touch with the situation. Later during an enemy counter attack when the troops on his left fell back he moved his Company forward under a very heavy enemy barrage to a position where they protected the Brigade flank. He also collected a number of men who were retiring and reorganised them in a defensive line which eventually checked and localised the enemy's attack. His initiative and courage at a critical time was most marked.

2373 Sergeant AFFLECK, Alexander James, M.M.

M.M.—For conspicuous gallantry and devotion to duty during the operations East of HAMEL, from 8-11/8/'18. This N.C.O. acted as Coy. Scout Sergt., and throughout the operation materially assisted his Coy. to keep direction through difficult country. In one velley he himself captured 15 prisoners who were escaping. On reaching the objective he assisted in forming his Coy. on its correct alignment.

M.M.—For bravery in the Field.

1059 Sergeant ALABASTER, William, M.M.

M.M.—For bravery in the Field.

Lieut.-Colonel ALLEN, Arthur Samuel, D.S.O., C. de G. (French), (M.I.D.)

D.S.O.—For conspicuous gallantry and devotion to duty. He led his Company with great dash and determination against enemy trenches through heavy artillery and machine-gun barrage, and against a stubborn resistance of the garrison, of whom he captured 100 prisoners. He continued to rally and lead his men to the attack, gaining further ground by his aggressive spirit, and setting a fine example of initiative and organising ability.

Lieut. ALLMAN, John Tilliard, M.M.

M.M.—For great bravery in an assault on German strong point and trench at GUEUDECOURT on the morning of 21/2/1917. He participated in the rush upon the strong point and also displayed great gallantry in the bombing operations along the trench. Later he acted with coolness and courage in the repulse of an enemy counter attack and though wounded in the hand by a hostile grenade, remained at his post for several hours.

Captain ANDERSON, Joseph Ringland, M.C.

M.C.—For conspicuous gallantry and devotion to duty during the attack West of BELLENGLISE, North of ST. QUENTIN, on 18th September, 1918. During a protracted advance he established his R.A.P. well forward in the open, and continued with cool courage to attend the wounded under heavy shell fire. His efforts saved many lives.

2123 L/Cpl. ANNAN, Francis Clifford, M.M.

M.M.—For conspicuous gallantry and devotion to duty during the operations East of HAMEL, East of CORBIE from 8th to 11th August, 1918.
During the advance while in charge of a Lewis Gun Section this N.C.O. did remarkably fine work. At one point one of the tanks was put temporarily out of action by enemy machine gun fire. He immediately rushed his guns forward and so skilfully engaged them that they were put out of action and captured. The advance then continued, many lives being saved.

3229 Private ANSELL, Thomas, M.M.

M.M.—For gallantry and devotion to duty during the operation near DERNANCOURT, South West of ALBERT, on 5th April, 1918. This man was a stretcher bearer. During the heavy barrage on the morning of the 5th April, 1918, he went out at great personal risk, bandaged wounded and brought them to cover. He followed up the attack in the afternoon amidst terrific M.G. fire and brought a number of wounded to places of safety. He worked hard all night bringing in wounded from NO MAN'S LAND at very great personal risk.

1309 Sergeant ASLATT, Harold Francis, D.C.M., M.M., M.S.M.

D.C.M.—For conspicuous devotion to duty during the attack West of BELLENGLISE on the 12th September, 1918. After the carrying parties for the two Stokes' Mortars became disconnected owing to fog, he went out and found them, getting the ammunition to the objective as soon as same was gained. During the exploiting patrol work in the afternoon of the 18th he kept touch with the two sections of guns and saw that ammunition was kept up to the mortars. During the operation of the 19th September, on hearing that bombs and S.A.A. were wanted to the front he, on his own initiative, gathered as many men as he could find and took charge of them, forming a carrying party and gathering ammunition up so that the attacking parties could have a plentiful supply ensuring a successful operation. During the whole of the operations his total disregard for danger, especially machine gun fire, coupled with his cheerful and energetic manner set an example which had good effects on all around him.

1309 Sergeant ASLATT, Harold Francis, D.C.M., M.M., M.S.M.

M.M.—For conspicuous gallantry and valuable service in command of a Mortar near ALBERT on 5th April, 1918, when his fire broke up several enemy attacks though his detachment were exposed to heavy M.G. and trench mortar fire throughout the day. He carried out his work as if on parade at a practice shoot and gave great assistance to the Infantry. In order to direct fire to the best advantage he repeatedly exposed himself to close range musketry. Sgt. ASLATT has been recommended for M.S.M. in King's Birthday Honours Despatch.

1309   Sergeant ASLATT, Harold Francis, D.C.M., M.M., M.S.M.

M.S.M.—For continuous good and gallant service in the field with the Battery since July, 1916. He has particularly distinguished himself by his zeal and devotion to duty in maintaining the supply of ammunition under fire and in circumstances of great difficulty.

This N.C.O. has set a particularly valuable example to his comrades by the cool and cheery manner in which he has carried out difficult and dangerous duties in the line as well as by his work as an Instructor out of the line. Period covered from 23rd September, 1917, to 25th February, 1918.

4488   Sergeant BAILEY, Arthur Edward Henry, M.M.

M.M.—For conspicuous gallantry in an attack on enemy strong point and trenches at GUEUDECOURT on the morning of 21/2/1917. After the section leader had been wounded he assumed command and acted with pluck and initiative. In bombing operation along the trench he acted as first bayonet man for awhile whilst directing the bombers as well. He also displayed great energy and coolness in the subsequent consolidation of the position

4489   C.S.M. BAILEY, Edgar Leslie, M.M.

M.M.—For bravery in the Field.

1912   Corporal BANNISTER, William Joseph, D.C.M.

D.C.M.—On April 5th, 1918, near DERNANCOURT, during the enemy attack T/Cpl. BANNISTER was in charge of a Lewis Gun under extremely heavy shell and M.G. fire. The enemy was advancing in force, but out of the field of fire of his gun on the ground, he mounted his gun on another man's shoulder and opened fire, inflicting heavy casualities on the enemy, holding up the advance for two hours and covering the withdrawal of our men to a better defensive position. In so doing he exposed himself to a very heavy concentration of shell and M.G. fire. Though twice wounded (in leg and arm) he carried on until wounded a third time more seriously. He was then forced to hand over his gun to his comrade. His main thought then was for the wounded of his section, and he refused to be removed until he saw that every man of his Section had been carried away.

Consequently in the withdrawal he had to be left behind, but was rescued four hours later when the Battn. made a counter attack and re-took the position. But for the courage and determination of this N.C.O. which held up the enemy advance for about two hours the enemy would have broken through before the other Companies had reached the position and consolidated it. His work during the whole tour was of the same exemplary nature.

Lieut. BARBER, Cecil, M.M.

M.M.—For great coolness and courage when observing from the roof of a house in the front line on 2/5/1918, under heavy fire near VILLERS BRETONNEUX, East of AMIENS. He obtained valuable information regarding enemy trenches and new works, which was of great use in bringing artillery fire to bear on important posts. The house was continually under artillery and very heavy M.G. fire. During the whole tour in the line he was on duty at this spot continuously from dawn to dark and displayed great zeal and ability in supplying information that enabled the artillery and M.G. fire to be directed on important enemy targets. He also did very valuable patrol work on the nights 29/4/'18 and 1/5/'18, when with great coolness and courage he patrolled very close to the enemy's positions and brought back valuable information regarding his dispositions.

4141 Private BASHAM, Maynard, M.M.

M.M.—For his courage and initiative whilst on patrol duty in DERNANCOURT, South West of ALBERT, on night of April 1st, 1918. This man was a member of a patrol sent out to reconnoitre DERNANCOURT after the hurricane bombardment. On reaching the outskirts of the village the patrol was halted by a German post guarding the archway leading to the road. Without hesitation he rushed the post causing the Bosche to retreat and allowing the patrol to proceed and obtain further information. But for his presence of mind the position would have become impossible. This man has on many occasions displayed marked courage.

7472 Sergeant BEAN, Vere Jack, D.C.M.

D.C.M.—For conspicuous gallantry and devotion to duty on all occasions.

During operations in April at DERNANCOURT when the Battn. was in the front line, BEAN showed conspicuous bravery and determination in conducting limbers of rations and wiring material to the line under heavy shell fire and over rough country. His example of coolness was a great support to the limber drivers. He did exceptionally good work in clearing the Bn. Quartermaster's Store from HENENCOURT during an enemy barrage on 5th April.

On the 7th May when entrusted to place two travelling kitchens near VILLERS BRETTONEUX the position was heavily shelled and, although his horse was killed beneath him he withdrew the kitchens and teams to safety. Cpl. BEAN'S reliable and continuous good work at all times is of great assistance and deserving of great praise. The period covered in the above recommendation is from February 16/17th September, 1918.

2143 L/Cpl. BELL, George Herbert, M.M.

M.M.—For his bravery and devotion to duty while his company was advancing to reinforce firing line after enemy attack near DERNANCOURT South West of ALBERT, on March 28th, 1918. Under very heavy barrage he carried wounded men to shelter and although himself loaded with Lewis Gun Panniers of his own section he carried for the gun of a section whose crew were all casualties.

4491 Corporal BENNETT, Herbert Bright, M.M.

M.M.—For his devotion to duty and splendid example set to his men during the attack West of BELLENGLISE on the 18/9/1918. He advanced in face of heavy machine gun fire in support of Infantry who were held up and brought his Mortar into action, firing on and silencing an active enemy machine gun thereby enabling the Infantry to push forward.

3113 L/Cpl. BICKERSTAFF, Herbert, M.M.

M.M.—For his conspicuous bravery and devotion to duty during our counter attack near DERNANCOURT on April 5th, 1918. This man at great personal risk rushed forward with L/Cpl. LOOLONG under very heavy artillery and M.G. barrage and captured a British Lewis Gun which was in the hands of the enemy and causing considerable damage to his Company and hindering the advance. The capture of this gun enabled the company to gain its objective with fewer casualties. This man continued to do excellent work until relieved.

2333 Private BIRKS, Arthur Horace, M.M.

M.M.—For conspicuous gallantry and devotion to duty during the operations East of HAMEL, East of CORBIE, from 8th to 11th August, 1918.

This soldier is a stretcher bearer, and during the consolidation of the objective his company was heavily shelled from the left and casualties were incurred. This soldier worked unceasingly with utter disregard for personal safety till all the wounded were evacuated, despite the fact that he himself was slightly wounded.

1728 Private BLACKBURN, Jeff, M.M.

M.M.—For conspicuous gallantry during our attack on MUN-STER ALLEY on the afternoon 7th August, 1916, in that he held back the enemy with bombs whilst a block was being built at the head of the trench. Military Medal awarded 28th August, 1916.

710 Sergeant BLENKINSOP, John David, MM.

M.M.—On the nights of the 19th and 20th August, 1915, Sgt. BLENKINSOP (then a Corporal of "D" Coy., 13th Battn., A.I.F.) was sent out to gain information as to the nature of the country in front, in view of an attack by the 13th Battn. on the 21st August. This work was carried out by him very skilfully in face of considerable danger, and the information gained was of considerable use in the attack that followed.

3015 L/Cpl. BLUNDEN, Thomas Henry, M.M.

M.M.—For consistent good work and devotion to duty during attacks on the enemy trenches at GUEUDECOURT on the morning of 21/2/'17 and the night of 22/23rd February, 1917. He was a member of a Lewis Gun Team and sent out in NO MAN'S LAND to cover our attack and did excellent work. At the time of the second attack Pte. BLUNDEN was suffering from very bad feet and the N.C.O. in charge of the gun wanted to substitute another man; Pte. BLUNDEN, however, insisted in taking part in the attack. Notwithstanding the very heavy state of the ground he stuck to his gun until relieved in the morning. This man by his courage and determination when he was practically unfit, set a splendid example to the remainder of the gun crew.

1879 L/Cpl. BLYTON, Charles Henry, M.M.

M.M.—For conspicuous gallantry and devotion to duty. During the advance West of BELLENGLISE on the 18th September, 1918, he greatly assisted in rushing a strong enemy post where many prisoners were taken, after putting up a determined fight. He took command of a Lewis Gun Section after the leader had become a casualty and handled them skilfully during the remainder of the action. Though buried by a shell and slightly wounded he refused to leave his platoon and continued, although suffering considerably.

3017 Sergeant BODYCOTE, Claude Edrick, M.M.

M.M.—For conspicuous gallantry and devotion to duty during the operations East of HAMEL, from 8-11/8/'18. This N.C.O. led his section through SUSAN WOOD mopping up about 20 of the enemy. Later he patrolled a huge dump in NO MAN'S LAND and brought back useful information.

3689 L/Cpl. BOND, William Henry, M.M.

M.M.—For courage and determination shown by him in an attack upon enemy strong point and trench at GUEUDECOURT on the morning of 21/2/'17. He acted with skill and coolness as a bomb thrower in the progress along the trench and, owing to this tenacity of purpose was one of the first to reach the objective where he showed great bravery in the face of a German counter bombing attack.

3719 Corporal BOSWELL, William Walter, M.M. and 2 Bars.

M.M.—From 5th to 8th August he worked unceasingly day and night carrying wounded near POZIERES. He particularly distinguished himself on the afternoon of 7th August, during the attack on MUNSTER ALLEY and TOOR TRENCH, when for three hours he bandaged wounded men and carried them as far as the Aid Post. All this time there was a heavy bombardment, and at places the communication trenches were blown in necessitating the Stretcher Bearers going overland.

3719 Corporal BOSWELL, William Walter, M.M. and 2 Bars.

Bar to M.M.—For his gallant conduct and untiring energy in collecting and attending the wounded during the enemy attack near DERNANCOURT, South West of ALBERT, on April 5th. He showed great courage in organising his stretcher bearers, seeking out the wounded, carrying them to safety and tending their wounds. Under very heavy artillery fire he worked for hours without a thought of his own safety and by his gallant conduct undoubtedly saved a number of lives. It was due to his effort that the wounded of his unit were cleared of the battlefield and his determined endurance had a very inspiring effect on all the men in his Battalion. 2nd Bar to M.M.—For conspicuous bravery and devotion to duty. On the morning of 18/9/1918 his Battn. was attacking West of BELLENGLISE. This N.C.O., who was in charge of stretcher bearers remained in a heavy barrage dressing and assisting wounded. His unfaltering courage not only prompted the admiration of the wounded, but his care and attention was of inestimable benefit to the men.

Lieut. BOWDEN, Robert, M.C.
M.C.—For conspicuous gallantry and devotion to duty in handling his platoon with great skill during the attack West of BELLENGLISE on the 18th September, 1918. A nest of machine guns caused great trouble. This Officer rushed forward with a few of his men, shot two of the enemy with his revolver, and captured 30 prisoners and a machine gun. Besides a number of machine guns his platoon secured 100 prisoners, two field guns, and three trench mortars.

2337 C.S.M. BRADFORD, James, D.C.M.
D.C.M.—For great coolness and resourcefulness under very trying circumstances during the night 29/30th August, 1916, when he was on duty in the front line at POZIERES The portion of the front line in which C.S.M. BRADFORD was stationed was subjected to a severe hostile artillery bombardment; owing to the heavy rain the trench was knee deep in water and portions of it were being continually blown in. C.S.M. BRADFORD spent the whole night moving along the trench encouraging the men in repairing the damaged trench. The cheerfulness and confidence displayed by him greatly assisted in steadying the men.

1678 C.S.M. BULL, Walter Davis, M M.
M.M.—For bravery and devotion to duty.

4152 Private BUSHELL, Ray Wilberforce, M.M.
M.M.—For gallantry and devotion to duty at ZONNEBEKE on the 12th October, 1917, during heavy enemy barrage and attack when the situation was obscure he went out on several occasions and repaired broken wires thus enabling communications to be maintained with the front line.

4747 C.S.M. CAMERON, James Gerald, D.C.M.
D.C.M.—For conspicuous bravery and devotion to duty during the attack West of BELLENGLISE on the 18th September, 1918. He was Scout N.C.O. On the Battalion reaching the objective he took forward an exploiting patrol with a Lewis Gun. He came in touch with three 5.9 Howitzers and their crew. He rushed the crews, six of the enemy being killed and 14 captured. The horses were killed and, owing to this the guns were captured.

1741 L/Cpl. CASEY, Patrick, M.M.
M.M.—Who was a Company Runner during the period 5th till 8th August, 1916 at POZIERES. He continuously carried messages, and at times had to pass through heavy shell fire. There was no communication trench, and he had to travel across open country, yet he succeeded in delivering his messages.

1890 L/Sgt. CASSELL, George Walter, M.M.
M.M.—At ZONNEBEKE on 12th October, 1917, he was in charge of the Company stretcher bearers and worked continuously with little food and no sleep, bandaging, and carrying wounded men through heavy shell and M.G. fire from NO MAN'S LAND. During enemy counter attack when the supply of stretchers gave out he organised squads of German prisoners and made them carry wounded back on blankets.
His courage and devotion to duty were the means of saving many valuable lives.

4017 L/Cpl. CAUGHEY, John, M.M.
M.M.—For bravery in the Field and devotion to duty.

5355 Corporal CHAMBERLAIN, Thomas, M.M.
M.M.—For conspicuous gallantry and devotion to duty during the attack West of BELLENGLISE on the 18/9/1918. He was No. 1 of a Lewis Gun, and when right of the company showed signs of being held up, he dashed forward into our barrage with his gun and brought enfilade fire to bear on a large body of the enemy. His action enabled his company to advance and capture those of the enemy who were not killed.

Lieut. CHEW, Albert Norman, C. de G. (Belgium), (M.I.D.)
M.I.D.—For great personal courage, initiative and devotion to duty at ZONNEBEKE on 12th October, 1917. During severe enemy barrage and counter attack when most of the posts were blown in and many of the officers and men had become casualities he reorganised the posts, supervised the supply of ammunition, regardless of personal safety. His timely action was instrumental in restoring the morale of his shaken unit.

2477 Sergeant CLARE, Thomas William, M.M.
M.M.—For conspicuous gallantry at GUEUDECOURT on the morning of 21st February, 1917, during an attack on enemy's strong point and trenches. He was in command of a squad of men with blankets to throw over the enemy's wire. He went forward under cover of the Stokes Gun barrage and took up a position close to the enemy's wire to watch the result of the Stokes shells to select a damaged point to rush. Immediately the barrage lifted he rushed forward under enemy rifle and bomb fire and successfully threw blankets over their wire. By his coolness and utter disregard for danger he greatly assisted the attacking party in entering the enemy's trench without delay.

1683 L/Cpl. CLARK, William Henry, M.M.
M.M.—On the night 15/16th October, 1916, during a raid on the German trenches near DIEPENDAAL, he was one of the bombing section under L/Cpl. VENABLES. The remainder of the section being delayed by wire. He displayed coolness and bravery in helping the Cpl. to carry out the work the section were detailed to do.

3042 Private CLARKE, Australia Rangy Jerome, M.M.
M.M.—For conspicuous gallantry and devotion to duty during operations East of HAMEL, East of CORBIE, 8-11/8/'18. This soldier acted as a Company Runner throughout the operations doing splendid work on every occasion. On the night 9-10/8/'18 he gallantly carried very important messages through heavy machine gun fire. His courage and initiative were beyond all praise.

2152 L/Cpl. COLLIVER, Walter, M.M.
M.M.—For gallantry at ZONNEBEKE on night of 12/13th October, 1917, during enemy counter attack when the Battn. left flank was threatened. He went forward under a very heavy enemy barrage to the left flank and ascertained the exact position. The information gained was of the greatest assistance to his Company Commander at a critical time.

984 Sergeant COOMBES, Robert Allen, M.M.
M.M.—For bravery in the Field and devotion to duty.

Captain CORNISH, Edmund Warhurst, M.C. and Bar.
M.C.—For conspicuous gallantry in leading an attacking party on enemy's strong point and trenches at GUEUDECOURT on the morning of the 21/2/'17. Lieut CORNISH was in charge of an attacking party. On the signal to attack he led his men with splendid dash and determination over enemy's wire and bombed the enemy out of his strong point. On this being attained he continued along the enemy's trench at the head of his men and bombed his way for a distance of 250 yards, killing and wounding many of the enemy and capturing 29 prisoners. Although seriously wounded he remained in the captured trench until the same was

consolidated. For three nights previous to this attack Lieut.
CORNISH had personally reconnoitred the strong point and NO
MAN'S LAND in the vicinity immediate, and the information he
had gained (under very dangerous conditions) was largely instrumental to the success of the attack.

Captain CORNISH, Edmund Warhurst, M.C. and Bar.

Bar to M.C.—East of ZONNEBEKE on 12th October, 1917, this
Officer successfully organised and personally supervised the laying
of the jumping off tapes in NO MAN'S LAND. At the time the
enemy artillery was extremely active and the tapes were repeatedly
broken by enemy shells. On the same evening acting as Brigade
representaive in the front area he skilfully stopped a retirement of
of a neighbouring unit which left the flank of this Brigade in a pre-
carious condition. His good judgment and initiative saved what
might have been a serious situation and is deserving of the highest
praise.
Has been awarded the Military Cross.

Lieut. COWARD, Harry Keith, D.C.M., M.C. and Bar.

M.C. (whilst seconded with 12/L.T.M.B.)—For conspicuous gallantry and devotion to duty, in following up the barrage in front
of our attacking troops and bringing fire to bear on strong enemy
points. His prompt action enabled our attack to go forward. He
afterwards commanded his guns under continuous heavy enemy
bombardment, setting a fine example to his men throughout the
whole of the operations.

Lieut. COWARD, Harry Keith, D.C.M., M.C. and Bar.

Bar to M.C. (whilst seconded with 12/L.T.M.B.)—For conspicuous
gallantry and devotion to duty, during operations West of BELLEN-
GLISE on the 18th September, 1918. It was due to this Officer's
gallant leadership and utter disregard for personal safety that the
Stokes Mortars under his charge were in postion in time to support the Infantry during consolidation of the first objective. During the succeeding phases of the operation he had his guns amongst
the first wave of the Infantry, and was able to silence hostile
machine guns which were causing casualities and holding up the
advance. In the final stage he had his two guns set up to protect
the left flank of the attacking Battn. whilst the mopping up process was in progress. The untiring energy and cheerful disposition
displayed by Lieut. COWARD undoubtedly assisted materially
to the success of the operations.

3366 Private COX, Thomas John, M.M.

M.M.—For bravery in the Field.

2/Lieut. CROOKS, Thomas Ray, M.C.

M.C.—For gallantry and devotion to duty at GUEUDECOURT
on the morning of the 21/2/'17 and the night of the 23-24/2/'17
during the attacks on enemy's strong points and trenches. C.S.M.
CROOKS was in charge of the carrying parties, carrying grenades and rifle grenades to the attacking troops. By his coolness
under heavy fire, combined with organisation and method he enabled a plentiful supply of grenades to be kept up, notwithstanding
the fact that conditions were abnormal as most of the carrying had
to be done through mud, knee deep. On both occasions he con-
trolled his parties through NO MAN'S LAND and the work done
by this W.O. at a critical time was magnificent.

5352 Private CUDDEFORD, Edgar Lewis, M.M.

M.M.—For bravery and devotion to duty during attack of 18th
September, 1918, an old British Outpost line near LE VERGUIER
Pte. CUDDEFORD, is a Battn H.Q. Runner, and during the advance, continually carried messages under adverse and most trying circumstances to various portions of the attacking line, always
returning and giving voluntary and correct information of the situation. During consolidation and after, owing to casualities in
runners, Pte. CUDDEFORD on numerous occasions volunteered to

take messages, always proving most reliable and cheerfully carrying out his duties.

4166   Hon./Sgt. CURRAN, Charles Ernest, M.M.
M.M.for his courage and disregard of danger —during enemy attack near DERNANCOURT, South West of ALBERT, on 5th April, 1918. Under terrific fire (rifle) and artillery fire this N.C.O. carried wounded men to the R.A.P. His work inspired the remainder of the stretcher bearers and earned the praise and confidence of his company.

1706   Sergeant CURSON, Edward Ernest, M.M.
M.M.—For meritorious services and devotion to duty near POZIERES from August 5th to 8th, 1916. During most of that period the trenches were subjected to a very heavy bombardment. When his section commander was killed, he acted on his own initiative and took charge and superintended the repairing of the damaged trenches. By his courage and cheerfulness he got the utmost out of his men.

3133   T/Cpl. DAVIDSON, Charles, M.M.
M.M.—For conspicuous gallantry and devotion to duty during the attack West of BELLENGLISE on the 18/9/'18. As platoon scout he went forward and found gaps in the wire for his platoon to pass through. When enemy dug-outs were reached he was al ways first on the spot and prevented the enemy putting up any defence. His courage and coolness were remarkable throughout the action.

1903   Corporal DAVIDSON, Ralph, M.M.
M.M.—For bravery in the Field and devotion to duty.

Captain DAVIES, Ernest, M.C.
M.C.—For consistent good work and ability as a Company Commander throughout the operations of his Battn. in France. His conduct in the Field has been marked by single-minded devotion to duty no less than by his thorough command of his men. Capt. DAVIES has repeatedly shown coolness and excellent judgment in action, coupled with a cheery disregard of personal danger, that have earned him the confidence and respect of all ranks in the Battalion.
Period covered from 23rd September, 1917, to 25th February, 1918.

3983   Private DAWSON, William Petrie, M.M.
M.M.—For coolness and devotion to duty shown by him on the afternoon of 15th August at POZIERES, when owing to heavy hostile artillery fire, the wires connecting 45th Battn. and 45th Battn. Headquarters were cut. Notwithstanding the heavy barrage, Pte. DAWSON was successful in establishing communication.

4761   L/Cpl. DE BELIN, George Arthur, M.M.
M.M.—For gallant conduct as a stretcher bearer during the attack near DERNANCOURT, South West of ALBERT, on March 28th, 1918. Prior to the enemy launching his attack, a heavy artillery barrage was put down on our lines causing many casualities in DE BELIN'S Company. He showed a disregard for the enemy's fire, and with untiring energy he sought out the wounded and conveyed them to safety. By his courage and skill he saved a number of lives and his endurance was extremely commendable.

4765   T/Dvr. DENZEL, Albert, M.M.
M.M.—For conspicuous gallantry and devotion to duty near LIHONS, South of VILLERS BRETONNEUX on 19/8/'18, at 8.30 p.m. The enemy attacked the Canadians on our right flank. This soldier was a member of a Lewis Gun team, and after No. 1 had been killed he took charge of the gun. In spite of a heavy M.G. and artillery barrage he daringly occupied a commanding position. Using his gun with remarkable skill and initiative he succeeded in enfilading the enemy's right flank causing many casualities among the attacking enemy force. The promptness and fine

fighting spirit shown by Pte. DENZEL set a splendid example to the men about him.

371   Sergeant DOIG, William Scotland, M.M. (M.I.D.)

M.M.—For exceptional bravery in carrying messages from supports to firing line during an attack on Hill 60 by the 13th Battn., A.I.F., on August 21st, 1915.

He was mentioned in despatches for the above on January 28th, 1916.

3910   L/Cpl. DREW, Leslie Sumner, M.M.

M.M.—For conspicuous bravery and devotion to duty at MOLENASRELSTHOEK on 30th September, 1917. Pte. DREW maintained the wires from his Company H.Q. to Battn. H.Q. throughout an enemy barrage and continuous heavy shelling. His work had to be done under direct observation of the enemy, and snipers were continuously firing at him during his work. By his perseverance and devotion to duty communications were maintained throughout. Later he was wounded by a sniper's bullet whilst carrying out line repair work.

3984   Corporal DRYER, John, M.M.

M.M.—For bravery in the Field and devotion to duty.

2148   Private DUFFY, Michael, M.M.

M.M.—For conspicuous gallantry and devotion to duty during the operations East of HAMEL, East of CORBIE, from 8th to 11th August, 1918. This soldier is a Company Scout, and throughout the attack was in front of his Company. At one point he attacked with great daring single-handed and captured 10 prisoners. Later during a minor operation when his Company advanced 1000 yards he acted as part of a screen and secured valuable information for his Company Commander. At all times he is a bold and fearless scout, and he set a splendid example of coolness and bravery during the whole operation.

1940   Private DUNCAN, Arthur, M.M. (M.I.D.)

M.M.—For bravery in the Field and devotion to duty.

2172   L/Cpl. EWENS, Wallace Wilfred, M.M.

M.M.—For conspicuous gallantry and devotion to duty during the attack West of BELLENGLISE on the 18/9/'18. He commanded a Lewis Gun Section, and on one occasion pushed his gun well forward against a strong point. He rushed the position, and 30 prisoners were captured. His conduct throughout the whole operation was of the highest order and added greatly to the success of the operation.

Captain FERGUSON, Leon Dudley, M.C.

M.C.—For gallantry and devotion to duty at GUEUDECOURT on the night of the 22/23rd February, 1917, during an attack on the enemy's trenches. Lieut. FERGUSON was in charge of the attacking party and led his men with great dash and determination, taking and holding 120 yards of enemy's trench, capturing 30 prisoners and inflicting numerous casualities on the enemy. This Officer by his utter disregard of danger and initiative rendered valuable service in the consolidation of the captured trench—a very difficult operation owing to the abnormal state (thigh deep in mud) and the darkness of the night.

Lieut. FITZHARDINGE, Augustus Clive B., M.C.

M.C.—For gallantry, bravery and initiative during the attack near LE VERGUIER, September 18th, 1918. Lieut. FITZHARDINGE as Transport Officer, was instrumental in the supply of S.A.A. and trench mortar ammunition provided most successfully by the working of pack mules under the direct supervision of this Officer. During the whole of the attack under trying and difficult circumstances, he made repeated trips with pack mules and limbers to Battn. H.Q. and the front line, often under considerable shell and M.G. fire. He was solely responsible for establishing and maintaining supplies to Battn. Dump. The loyalty and good work of Lieut. FITZHARDINGE during the operation was most conspicuous.

Lieut. FROST, Gerald Alfred John, **M.M.**

M.M.—For bravery in the Field and devotion to duty.

2833 L/Cpl. GEARY, Peter Bernard, **M.M.**

M.M.—For conspicuous gallantry and devotion to duty during the attack West of BELLENGLISE on 18/9/'18. His section suffered heavy casualities during an enemy barrage and became isolated. Although wounded, this N.C.O. rallied his men and led them forward until so badly wounded a second time that he was unable to proceed. His conduct was an admirable example to the men.

3525 Private GIBSON, William, **M.M.**

M.M.—For courage and devotion to duty on the night of 2/3rd May, near VILLERS BRETONNEUX, East of AMIENS. When all telephone lines with the front were broken he worked continuously all night under very heavy shell fire repairing the lines and succeeded in keeping Battn. H.Q. in communication with the front line thereby enabling information of the greatest value to be transmitted without delay. His work during the whole tour showed great keenness and utter disregard for personal safety.

2/Lieut. GOCHER, William Whitley, **M.M. and Bar.**

M.M.—On the night of 15/16th October, 1916, during a raid on the German trenches near DIEPENDAAL. He was in charge of the bombers and displayed great coolness and aggressiveness in handling his party. Also when returning, although wounded himself, was of great assistance in bringing in one of our men who had been badly wounded.

2/Lieut. GOCHER, William Whitley, **M.M. and Bar.**

Bar to M.M.—For exceptional gallantry and leadership on the morning of the 21st February, 1917, at GUEUDECOURT, during an attack on an enemy's strong point and trenches. Sgt. GOCHER led his team of bombers against a strong point and after same was bombed and captured, he continued the attack up the enemy's trenches. As the trench was practically impassable owing to the mud, he led his men along the parapet regardless of heavy M.G. fire. On reaching the objective he immediately organised a team of rifle grenadiers and kept the Germans back until the block was put in. He remained in charge of his bombing team at the block until the night 22/23rd February, 1917, and then took an active part in capturing another 120 yards of trench. The dash, determination, and coolness, under fire, shown by this N.C.O. was very marked, and the example he set to his men was splendid.

2913 Sergeant GOLDEN, James Edward Joseph, **D.C.M.**

D.C.M.—For conspicuous gallantry and ability in leading his platoon throughout the operation East of HAMEL, East of COR BIE, on 8th August, 1918. During the advance he rushed the crews of two guns capturing them intact. After reaching the objective he pushed forward with a Lewis Gun patrol to engage a field gun which was firing with open sights. This he did so effectively that the gun was put out of action, thus preventing casualties.

2182 Sergeant GOSPER, Vincent James, **D.C.M.**

D.C.M.—For his splendid leadership, initiative and courage during the enemy attack near DERNANCOURT, South West of AL BERT, on April 5th, 1918. He was in charge of his platoon in the support line, when he received the report that the enemy was bombing the way up. He immediately rallied his platoon, pushed them to a position from which he gallantly defended his flank. By his disregard for heavy rifle and M.G. fire he kept his men under control and held up the advance of the enemy for 2 hours. When almost surrounded he again showed great skill in withdrawing his men, keeping them well in hand, and taking up his position again in the Reserve Line.

2181 L/Cpl. GREAR, William, **M.M.**

M.M.—For gallant conduct during an attack upon German strong point and trench at GUEUDECOURT, on the morning of 21/2/'17. The assault was delivered under cover of a barrage of Stokes Guns.

The position was protected by strong wire and before the Stokes had finished firing Pte. GREAR dashed forward with Sgt. CLARE and laid blankets across the wire to facilitate the progress of the storming party. He then returned for more blankets which he placed in position. Subsequently he rendered valuable assistance in the operations along the trench.

3479   Sergeant GREENWOOD, Arthur Lewis, D.C.M., M.M.

D.C.M.—For conspicuous gallantry and devotion to duty. As C.S.M. he has at all times inspired his men with confidence, and his courage and energy have materially assisted in the successful issue of operations. During the period under review, 25th February to 16/17 September, 1918, several attacks have been made, and on each occasion he has made himself conspicuous by his gallantry and devotion to duty.

3479   Sergeant GREENWOOD, Arthur Lewis, D.C.M., M.M.

M.M.—For conspicuous gallantry and devotion to duty, during operations East of HAMEL, from 8-11/8/'18. He acted as Coy. Sgt. Major throughout the operations. By his courage and energy he materially assisted in the success of his Company. Later, during a minor operation, when his company advanced the line 1000 yards he was in charge of the covering party and was wounded while rushing an enemy machine gun which was harrassing the company. Throughout the operation his conduct was beyond all praise.

2528   Private HAEBICH, Frank, D.C.M., M.M.

D.C.M.—For conspicuous bravery and leadership during the counter attack near DERNANCOURT, South West of ALBERT on the afternoon of 5th April, 1918. During the advance a German machine gun was giving considerable trouble to the attackers. Pte. HAEBACH realising the position gathered five men, and by skilful manoeuvre succeeded in capturing the gun thus enabling the attacking waves to reach their objective. This man continued to do excellent work until he was wounded later. His work has always been of the highest quality.

2528   Private HAEBICH, Frank, D.C.M., M.M.

M.M.—For bravery in the Field and devotion to duty.

3787   Corporal HAGGERWOOD, Frederick Isaac, M.M.

M.M.—For bravery in the Field and devotion to duty.

4197   Private HALL, Joseph, M.M.

M.M.—For his heroic action in rescuing a comrade during enemy attack near DERNANCOURT, South West of ALBERT on April 5th, 1918. After his company had withdrawn, Pte. HALL discovered that one of his section was missing. Without hesitation he ran out under a hurricane barrage of M.G. and shell fire a distance of 800 yards and carried back his mate to safety. Although exhausted he persisted in bandaging his mate and assisting in carrying him to the R.A.P. This set a fine example to his company of disregard for danger and devotion to duty.

1927   Sergeant HANCOCK, Phillip Austin, D.C.M.

D.C.M.—For conspicuous gallantry and good leadership during the attack of 18th September, 1918, near LE VERGUIER. Sgt. HANCOCK'S platoon was held up by a portion of enemy's trench which was being strongly defended. Sgt. HANCOCK was seen to go ahead of his platoon and jump into an occupied enemy trench which he proceeded to bomb. He captured 9 prisoners, and very considerably cleared the way for his platoon, taking control later when his Officer and Platoon Sergeant were wounded. Throughout the operation he set a very fine example, and rendered most valuable assistance.

2290   Private HARRIS, William Alexander Rencher, D.C.M.

D.C.M.—For conspicuous gallantry and great devotion to duty during the operations East of HAMEL, East of CORBIE, from 8th to 11th August, 1918. When his section commander became a casualty he immediately took command of the section and led them throughout the operation with great skill and dash. His section was the first to reach a battery of 5.9 inch guns which were still in action. These were quickly silenced and the crews captured. Later as patrol leader he did valuable work. A keen and resourceful soldier he set a magnificent example.

Lieut. HAZELWOOD, Frederick Henry, M.M.

M.M.—For distinguished gallantry and ability in command of a platoon near DERNANCOURT, South West of ALBERT, on 5th April, 1918, after his Officer had been killed early in the day. He selected sites for his men to dig in under heavy fire and succeeded in getting the work done quickly and well. But for the excellent example and leading of this N.C.O. the situation would have been by no means as secure as it was.

3809 Corporal HEMMING, George Harry, M.M.

M.M.—In recognition of gallant conduct and determination displayed in escaping, or attempting to escape. from captivity.

Brig.-General HERRING, Sydney Charles Edgar, C.M.G., D.S.O., C. de G. (French), Croix D'Officer (French), Legion of Honour (French), (5 M.I.D.)

C.M.G.—This Officer has commanded the 13th Australian Infantry Brigade with skill and resource since the 28th June, 1918, and especially during the week immediately prior to 18th September, 1918, when his Brigade, acting as advance guard to the Division was most skilfully handled by him, capturing considerable ground and prisoners. His work throughout (and especially during the period 18th September to 11th November, 1918) has been sound, skilful and reliable. He is worthy of high distinction.

Brig.-General HERRING, Sydney Charles Edgar, C.M.G., D.S.O., C. de G. (French), Croix D'Officer (French), Legion of Honour (French), (5 M.I.D.)

D.S.O.—For consistent, thorough, and good work in raising and training his Battalion and subsequently commanding it with conspicuous success in action near FLEURBAIX and at POZIERES from 5th to 15th August, and from 29th August to 2nd September. This Officer also served with distinction on GALLIPOLI where he gained the Legion of Honour, but no other reward.

3336 L/Cpl. HOCKING, Harold Jeffery, M.M.

M.M.—At DERNANCOURT, South West of ALBERT, on April 5th, 1918, during an enemy attack this N.C.O. displayed exceptional bravery and endurance in handling his Lewis Gun. The enemy was attacking under cover of an intense artillery and machine gun barrage. In order to bring more destructive fire to bear on the attacking Infantry this N.C.O. got out on the parapet and allowed his shoulder to be used as a stand for a Lewis Gun. Shortly afterwards the gunner was wounded, and L/Cpl. HOCKING then took the gun himself and firing from his shoulder as he would a rifle inflicted heavy loss on the enemy. His contempt for the enemy fire and his devotion to duty contributed a great deal toward breaking the enemy attacks on his Company's sector.

Captain HOLMAN, Jack Hilton, M.C. and Bar.

M.C.—For his splendid leadership, courage and devotion to duty during the enemy attack near DERNANCOURT, South West of ALBERT, 5th April, 1918. On the morning of 5th April, when the Battn. moved forward to meet the enemy attack Captain HOLMAN displayed great skill in handling the Company, and by his careful arrangement of position during a very heavy barrage avoided many casualties. Later when the Company was ordered to move forward this Officer organised and led his Company to the front line and took over the position. It was due to the careful organisation and strong control of the Company that there were not a number of casualties. He then went along his line, and both his example of courage and cheery words to his ment put fresh heart into them and immediately prepared them for a counter attack which he led at 5.15 p.m. In this attack he distinguished himself by his bravery, determination and dash. At this time he was the only Officer left in his Company. After taking his objective he sent useful information back to Battn. H.Q., and with very sound judgment consolidated the position, all the time cheering up his men and inspiring them with the determination to win. His general work during the whole tour was of the highest quality, and he was untiring in his efforts to do his duty under trying circumstances.

Captain HOLMAN, Jack Hilton, M.C. and Bar.

Bar to M.C.—During the attack West of BELLENGLISE, on the 18th September, he commanded the company on the right sector of his Battn front. Shortly after the advance commenced it was found that the Battn. on the right was unable to proceed. This menaced the advance of his Battn., but Capt. HOLMAN, although there were few reserves at his disposal, was able by his skill and judgment to not only avert disaster on the exposed flank, but allowed his Battn. to attain its objective in safety. His dispositions for this purpose were excellent. After arriving at the objective he displayed great gallantry in leading a small party beyond to attack the crew of a 5.9 battery, all of whom were killed or captured and the guns taken. His coolness and daring were a great incentive to all.

Lieut. HOPGOOD, Harry Parsons, D.C.M.

D.C.M.—For conspicuous gallantry and devotion to duty. Seeing that our advance was likely to be held up, he organised a party and attacked a strong point, capturing eleven prisoners. He showed great initiative and resource at a critical moment. He was wounded shortly afterwards.

1717   Sergeant HORTON, Sydney Frederick, M.M.

M.M.—During the operations East of HAMEL, East of CORBIE, on 8th August, 1918, this N.C.O. showed great dash and leadership. At JEAN WOOD his platoon rushed a battery of 77 mm. guns, capturing them, with two heavy M.G.'s with crews intact. This daring attack undoubtedly saved many casualities. He is a daring patrol leader, and at all times set a magnificent example of courage, initiative and determination.

Major HOWDEN, Harold Charles, M.C. and Bar.

M.C.—Near POZIERES, Capt. Harold Charles HOWDEN took over on the night of 5th August, 1916, an isolated position of the front line during a heavy hostile artillery bombardment; being warned by the Officer whom he relieved that he could expect a counter attack at daylight he immediately set to work to strengthen his position, and when the counter attack took place on the morning of the 6th, was successful in repulsing it. Owing to his thorough consolidation that portion of the line, notwithstanding an incessant bombardment, was successfully held.

Major HOWDEN, Harold Charles, M.C. and Bar.

Bar to M.C.—For gallantry and devotion to duty in reorganising and carrying out two attacks on an enemy's strong point and trenches at GUEUDECOURT on the morning of 21/2/'17 and night of 22-23/2/'17. Owing to the abnormal wet state of the trenches these attacks were carried out under great difficulty and the success of both attacks was largely due to Capt. HOWDEN'S organising ability and attention to details. On both occasions immediately the trenches were captured, Capt. HOWDEN took charge and organised their defense. As the result of both operations nearly 500 yards of enemy's trenches were captured and held, and 60 prisoners taken.

3338   Corporal HUGHES, Ernest Everitt, M.M. and Bar.

M.M.—For conspicuous gallantry and devotion to duty in an attack on enemy strong point and trench at GUEUDECOURT on the morning of 21/2/'17. He was in an exposed position above the parapet well to the flank of the leading party bombing along the trench. From there he indicated the enemy to our bombers and was instrumental in directing fire upon a number of the enemy who were attempting to take our bombers in flank. He displayed the utmost coolness throughout.

3338   Corporal HUGHES, Ernest Everitt, M.M. and Bar.

Bar to M.M.—For bravery in the field and devotion to duty.

1934 Sergeant HUNT, James, **M.M.**

M.M.—For conspicuous gallantry and devotion to duty during operations East of HAMEL, East of CORBIE, from 8th to 11th August, 1918. Throughout the operations he led his section with great skill capturing prisoners and a M.G. Later during a minor operation while his platoon was digging in, they were heavily engaged by M.G.'s and Trench Mortars. His utter disregard of danger had a great effect on his men, and the operation was completely successful. He is, at all times, a fearless and skilful leader.

2291 Private IRVIN, David Christian, **M.M.**

M.M.—For conspicuous ability during the operations East of HAMEL, East of CORBIE, on the 8th August, 1918. During the advance this soldier was one of the mopping-up party in CAROLINE WOOD. He came upon an enemy post in which were 7 Germans fully armed, including an Officer who was using a telephone. He called on them to surrender, but the Officer continued speaking in the telephone. He rushed the Officer and bayonetted him, and captured the remainder and saved many casualties from being inflicted on the Company. Throughout the operations his courage was beyond all praise.

3551 Sergeant JONES, Richard Ernest, **M.M.**

M.M.—For courage and devotion to duty during the attack on DERNANCOURT RIDGE, South West of ALBERT, on 5th April, 1918. When all the Officers near him were killed or wounded he rallied the men and led them on. He found that his left flank was exposed, so, taking some men from his second wave he made a defensive flank. By this act he averted what would have been a critical position. Although wounded he carried on until wounded a second time.

1852 L/Corporal KAMMELL, John Frederick, **M.M.**

M.M.—For great courage and devotion to duty during the attack on MONUMENT WOOD near VILLERS BRETONNEUX, East of AMIENS on the night 2/3rd May, 1918. Under a very heavy barrage he worked continuously repairing broken telephone lines and by his untiring energy and gallant conduct succeeded in maintaining communication with the front, thus enabling valuable information to be transmitted without delay. His disregard of the enemy fire was a splendid example to his comrades.

3358 T/C.S.M.—KEARNEY, Arthur Lionel, **M.M.**

M.M.—At GUEUDECOURT for conspicuous gallantry and promptitude in attacking and surprising an enemy patrol on the morning of 21st November, 1916. L/Cpl. KEARNEY was in charge of a Sector of GOODWIN'S Post at the time, and seeing this patrol approaching, allowed them to get within a few feet and then dispersed them with bombs, killing three and wounding several others. On the morning he killed another German who was approaching his post. A keen and brave fighter.

522 Sergeant KELLY, Charles Henry, **M.M.** (Serbian Gold Medal).

M.M.—For bravery in the Field and devotion to duty.

522 Sergeant KELLY, Charles Henry, **M.M.** (Serbian Gold Medal).

Serbian Gold Medal.—On the morning of the 6th August, at POZIERES, after a German counter attack had failed, Pte. KELLY, who is an excellent rifle shot, and a very cool and daring sniper, killed about a dozen Germans. He was at GALLIPOLI from the landing until wounded on August 21st, 1915. During the period he did excellent work as a sniper and scout.

1721 Corporal KING, William James, **M.M.**

M.M.—For devotion to duty while acting as a runner at POZIERES during period 5th till 8th August, 1916. During that time he was carrying messages from the front line to Battn. H.Q., and frequently had to pass heavy hostile artillery barrages.

Lieut. KIRKWOOD, John Barton, **D.C.M.** (M.I.D.)

D.C.M.—For conspicuous good work by day and night in front of line.

Lieut. KIRMAN, Joseph, **M.C., M.M.**

M.C.—For his gallantry and devotion to duty at ZONNEBEKE

on the night of 12-13/10/'17, during strong enemy counter attacks. When the unit on the left of the Brigade retired he placed his Lewis Guns in position to cover the subsequent retirement of the 48th and 47th A.I.F. Battalions. He then re-organised the Battn. front line under a very severe enemy barrage regardless of his own personal safety. During the whole period in the line from 9/10/'17 to 13/10/'17, though his Company lost all Officers, except himself, and the climatic conditions were most strenuous, his cheeriness and example at all times inspired all.

Major KNOX, George Edward, M.C.

M.C.—For general excellence, gallantry and devotion to duty since the formation of Units in March, 1916. By personal bravery, coolness and leadership he particularly distinguished himself in operations at POZIERES in August, 1916, and GUEUDECOURT January-February, 1917.

Lieut. KIRMAN, Joseph, M.C., M.M.

M.M.—Who, on night 1/2nd September, 1916, under heavy shell fire rendered valuable assistance to the Engineer Officers in constructing an assembly trench opposite MOUQUET FARM. Sgt. KIRMAN, by his coolness, was one of those responsible for the work being a success.

2043 Corporal LAGUTIN, Nicholas, M.M.

M.M.—For conspicuous gallantry and devotion to duty near LIHONS, South of VILLERS BRETONNEUX, from 15/8/'18 to 19/8/'18. This N.C.O. was in charge of a bombing block within 25 yards of the enemy. On the evening of the 16th the enemy under cover of bombs and rifle grenades made four distinct attempts to rush the post. Owing to the bravery and determination of this N.C.O. each attack was beaten off with loss to the enemy. He organised his bombers very skilfully and harassed the enemy unceasingly.

Lieut. LEDDY, Joseph, M.M.

For gallantry displayed on the night of the 6/7th August, 1915, when Platoon Sergeant of "A" Company, 13th Battn., A.I.F. During the night advance of the 4th Brigade on the date the platoon of which Sgt. LEDDY was Platoon Sergeant was ordered to clear the hill of snipers who were retarding the advance. Considerable opposition was encountered, and the Platoon Commander was severely wounded. Sgt. LEDDY displayed exceptional bravery and skill in handling his men, and successfully cleared the hill.

Major LEE, Joseph Edward, D.S.O., M.C., (2 M.I.D.)

D.S.O.—For great devotion to duty during the whole of the period this Officer has been with the Brigade, namely, about twelve months. His work in and out of action has been conspicuously good, and very valuable. During the most strenuous periods when active operations were in progress, he would never rest or go off duty, although often almost physically exhausted. His sound advice, tactical and otherwise, has always been of the greatest assistance, and his extremely daring and thorough reconnaissances have been invaluable.

Lieut. LIND, Ernest Edward, M.M.

M.M.—During the operations East of HAMEL, East of CORBIE, on 8th August, 1918, this N.C.O. showed great ability and courage. He was on the left flank of his Company and was responsible for keeping touch with the neighbouring units. This he very ably did. While passing through CAROLINE WOOD his platoon was fired on by machine guns that were protecting a 6in. naval gun. These he engaged with rifle grenades, and working round their flank rushed them. Crews and guns were captured intact.

Lieut. LISLE, Percy Albert, M.C.

M.C.—For conspicuous gallantry during the operations East of HAMEL, East of CORBIE on the 8th August, 1918. Throughout the attack he led his platoon with great dash and skill. When held up by enemy machine gun fire he gallantly advanced with his platoon and succeeded in capturing the machine guns and crews. By this daring action he prevented many casualties from being inflicted on his Company, and thus allowed the advance to continue. After the capture of the second objective he led a battle patrol with great pluck and determination, and by his resolute action dislodged the enemy post and gained the objective.

3177 Private LONG, Gilbert Joseph Aloysius, M.M.
M.M.—For courage and devotion to duty at ZONNEBEKE on 12th October, 1917. He was one of a party digging a communication trench during an attack on enemy trenches, and when the party was withdrawn, owing to very heavy casualities, he remained behind and dressed the wounded. He then organised stretcher squads and got all the wounded back. His courage under very heavy fire was most marked.

3364 Corporal LOO LONG, William, M.M. and Bar.
M.M.—For his splendid action and bravery during the counter attack near DERNANCOURT, South West of ALBERT on afternoon of 5th April, 1918. During the advance he displayed great courage and was instrumental in causing a number of casualities on the enemy. Later on in the advance this N.C.O. located a British Lewis Gun in German hands which was harassing our men. At great personal risk he, with a man of his section, rushed forward, killed two Germans and captured the gun. This N.C.O. has always shown considerable dash and courage.

3364 Corporal LOO LONG, William, M.M. and Bar.
Bar to M.M.—During the operations East of HAMEL, East of CORBIE, on 8th August, 1918, this N.C.O. conspicuously distinguished himself by outflanking a very active enemy M.G., thereby capturing it and the crew complete. Later on he made a valuable reconnaissance of NO MAN'S LAND.

Lieut. LOVE, James, M.M.
M.M.—On the night of 15/16th October, 1916, during a raid on the German trenches near DIEPENDAAL. He was in charge of a flank bombing party and displayed coolness, courage and resource in exploring the hostile trenches in his sector.

2971 Sergeant LOVETT, George, M.M.
M.M.—For bravery and devotion to duty at MOLENAARELSTHOEK on the night 28/29th September, 1917. This N.C.O. was in charge of a patrol which located a small hostile group in a pill box. By the skilful handling of his patrol he succeeded in driving the enemy out of the pill box and secured one slightly wounded German whom he brought back to our lines.

Lieut. LOWICK, John Warne, M.M.
M.M.—For his courage at ZONNEBEKE on 12th October, 1917. He went out on several occasions and repaired broken wires during a severe enemy barrage and counter attack. His coolness and determination was most marked and his perseverance in his duty enabled communication to be maintained at a critical time.

Lieut. MAIDEN, Herbert Edward, M.M.
M.M.—For good work done at POZIERES from 5th to 8th August, and also from the 28th to 31st August, 1916. During most of this period he was in charge of the Lewis Guns and displayed exceptional ability in handling his guns and crew under heavy shell fire. Frequently he was out in NO MAN'S LAND all night with his guns whenever an attack was imminent.

2941 Private MARRIOTT, William, M.M.
M.M.—For bravery and devotion to duty as a runner during the operations of the 5th April, 1918, at DERNANCOURT. He crossed through a very heavy barrage of shells and machine gun bullets many times with messages to the line. During the attack of the 5th April, when all communication with the advancing companies was cut he volunteered to find them, and after spending a considerable time in the open and under extremely heavy fire he got into touch with the companies and getting information from them brought it back to Battn. H.Q.

2/Lieut. MARSHALL, Henry Russell, M.M.
M.M.—On the night of 15/16th October, 1916, during a raid on the German trenches near DIEPENDAAL. He was in charge of

a section of bombers who were covering the retirement of the raiding party. He carried out his work very coolly and bravely and
was the last man to leave the hostile trenches.

3409   Private MATHEWS, Frederick, M.M.

M.M.—For conspicuous gallantry as a Company Stretcher Bearer
during the enemy attack near DERNANCOURT on March 28th,
1918. Prior to the enemy Infantry attack a heavy Artillery barrage
was placed on his Company Sector causing a number of casualties.
Disregarding the enemy's fire, Pte. MATHEWS sought out the
wounded, tended their wounds and carried them to a safe position.
His cheery disposition encouraged the men of his Company and his
devotion to duty undoubtedly saved a number of lives.

Lieut. MOORE, Basil Raymond, M.C.

For conspicuous gallantry and devotion to duty during the attack
West of BELLENGLISE on the 18th September, 1918. Lieut.
MOORE led his platoon in an assault in the face of heavy machine
gun fire from an old building surrounded by a hedge. Whilst Lewis
gunners engaged the enemy he led the remainder of his platoon
round the flank, and after killing several of the enemy, 55 prisoners and several machine guns were taken. His gallantry and skilful
leadership contributed largely to the success of his Company in
gaining the objective.

4517   Corporal MORGAN, Reuben, M.M.

M.M.—For his leadership, courage and devotion to duty whilst
on patrol duty in DERNANCOURT, South West of ALBERT,
night of 1st April, 1918. After reaching the nearest houses on the
outskirts of the village 2 machine guns concealed on the right of
the patrol opened fire, thus cutting the patrol off. This unforeseen
event placed the patrol in a tight corner and would have been dis-
astrous if it had not been for the presence of mind and initiative of
Cpl. MORGAN, who immediately rallied his section, crawled forward under heavy machine gun fire, and when 10 yards from the
guns threw bombs, blowing up the guns and saving the situation
from this flank.

4561   Private MORTIMER, Alfred, M.M.

M.M.—For conspicuous gallantry and devotion to duty during operations near HAMEL, East of CORBIE, from 8th to 11th
August, 1918. As platoon runner he carried out his duties
with great courage and energy, frequently passing through very
heavy machine gun and artillery barrages. Later, when he was
hit by a piece of shell he refused to leave his platoon and continued to carry out his duties. He is at all times a fine example to
his platoon and was exceptionally daring in his actions throughout the attack.

Lieut. MORTON, Victor, M.C.

M.C.—For conspicuous gallantry and devotion to duty near
HAMEL, East of CORBIE, on night 30th June and 1st July. Iden-
tification was urgently needed, and this Officer with eight men left
our lines to secure prisoners. Having proceeded about 700 yards
across NO MAN'S LAND a party of 30 of the enemy was observed working on a new trench. Quickly forming his plan of
attack this Officer led his men to the flank of the enemy party to
secure the greatest fire effect. On a pre-arranged signal the covering party opened fire, and he, with his Sergeant, rushed the nearest
Hun, seized him by each arm and brought him to our lines. The
operation was so vigorously carried out that it was completely successful. Casualties were inflicted on the enemy and our patrol was
unscathed. He showed courage and enterprise of a high order.

Lieut. MUIR, Alexander Roxburgh, M.C.

M.C.—For conpicuous gallantry and devotion to duty. He led his
platoon with great skill and determination capturing an enemy
strong point, which he re-organised and held. He afterwards did
most valuable work in extending his battalion front and in leading
a reconnoitring patrol into the enemy's country.

Lieut. MURRAY, Robert Andrew. Malcolm. M.C.

M.C.—For conspicuous gallantry and devotion to duty in assisting to take and hold enemy's strong hold and trenches at GUEUDE-COURT on the morning of 21/2/'17. Lieut. MURRAY led his men with great dash and determination, and after bombing up and capturing the enemy's trench he took charge and superintended the building of our block in same, this was done under enemy bomb fire. At daylight, under cover of our rifle grenade, he, on two separate occasions moved our block further along the enemy's trench and thus gained not only more trench, but a more advantageous position for the block. Although another Officer was sent down to relieve him next morning he refused to leave his post until he was quite satisfied that same was safe and secure. On three successive nights prior to the attack, he personally reconnoitred the enemy's position and wire and the information he gained was of great assistance to the attacking party. The coolness and utter disregard of danger shown by this Officer was largely instrumental in making the attack a success.

3853   Corporal MacGREGOR, Roderick Kenneth, M.M.
M.M.—For his courage and splendid example during an attack upon enemy trenches on the night of 22/23rd February, 1917, at GUEUDECOURT. At a critical moment when progress was almost impossible on account of the deep mud and the enemy were attempting to offer a stubborn resistance, he acted with great spirit and determination. He showed excellent leadership and his coolness under fire was admirable. Later he worked constantly in connection with the consolidation of the position.

2777   Private McBRIDE, Michael, M.M.
M.M.—For conspicuous courage and devotion to duty as a Stretcher Bearer during the operations near DERNANCOURT, South West of ALBERT, on the afternoon of 5th April, 1918. During very heavy bombardment this man, regardless of danger went forward into NO MAN'S LAND on several occasions attending to the wounded and bringing them back to safety. His determination set a fine example to the other bearers and earned confidence from all ranks of the Company.

5423   L/Cpl. McCUSKER, Hugh, M.M.
On the night of 15/16th October, 1916, during a raid on the German trenches near DIEPENDAAL, he was a Stretcher Bearer attached to the party. After carrying in one wounded man (on the back) from NO MAN'S LAND to our trenches, he returned with a stretcher for a second casualty.

2958   Corporal McDONALD, Frank Eugene, M.M.
M.M.—For conspicuous gallantry and devotion to duty. At one period during the advance West of BELLENGLISE on the 18/9/'18 the enemy was observed endeavouring to pull out his Batteries from the gun pits with horse transport. This N.C.O. was in charge of a Lewis Gun Section, promptly rushed his section forward in spite of heavy fire, and shot the horse teams, thus enabling the guns to be captured.

2002   Private McFADDEN, Frank Albert, M.M.
M.M.—At POZIERES, Pte. McFADDEN, who was employed as Battn. Runner between Headquarters and the firing line, was practically continuously on duty from the night of 5th August, 1916, until the afternoon of the 8th. A great deal of his work had to be done at night and under heavy hostile artillery fire. He carried out his duties with the greatest bravery and coolness, never failing to deliver his messages.

1696   Corporal McGREGOR, Sydney, M.M.
M.M.—For great gallantry and devotion to duty in an attack upon an enemy strong point and trench at GUEUDECOURT on the morning of 21/2/'17. Though wounded in the head with a bayonet in a hand-to-hand encounter he managed to kill his opponent. Subsequently he remained at his post until the objective had been reached and the position in course of consolidation, when he was ordered away by the officer on the spot.

Lieut. McKENZIE, John Reginald, M.M.
M.M.—For conspicuous bravery and coolness displayed by him when

on duty in the firing line at POZIERES on 6th and 7th August, 1916, when the line was subjected to a heavy bombardment. On one occrous occasions he has succeeded in bringing food and ammunition to the front line when it was thought to be impossible owing to heavy enemy barrages, and it has been due to his gallant conduct casion the trenches on our left were actually entered by Germans. Sgt. McKENZIE, by his good work did much to steady the men, and was of great assistance in holding the lines.

Lieut. McKINLEY, Thomas John, M.S.M.

M.S.M.—For consistent good work and devotion to duty as C.Q.M.S. and R.Q.M.S. throughout the operation of the Battalion in France. He has shown untiring energy and zeal in the performance of his duties, often under enemy fire, and has been of the greatest assistance in providing for the needs of the men in the line. Period covered from 23rd September, 1917, to 25th February, 1918.

Lieut. McMAHON, Randolph George F., M.C. (M.I.D.)

M.C.—For conspicuous gallantry and devotion to duty. He organised and skilfully led a counter-attack which drove back the enemy with heavy losses. He set a fine example of courage and initiative.

2378 Sergeant McMANUS, Marcus John, M.M.

M.M.—For conspicuous gallantry and devotion to duty during operations East of HAMEL, East of CORBIE, from 8th to 11th August, 1918. He acted as Company Sergeant-Major throughout the action and had command of the Headquarters platoon which he lead with great skill. At one point he captured 43 prisoners. Always cool and energetic he was a great assistance to his Company Commander.

Lieut. and Hon. Capt. NEAVES, Henry Herbert, M.C.

M.C.—For gallant conduct and great devotion to duty. On numand courage that all requirements for the front line have always reached their destination.

As Quartermaster, Lieut. NEAVES is always most conscientious and reliable, at all times showing great gallantry. The period covered in the above recommendation is from 25th February to 16th/17th September, 1918.

2463 Private NICOLLS, George Albert, M.M.

M.M.—For his determination and devotion to duty during attacks upon an enemy Strong Post and trenches at GUEUDECOURT from the 21st to the 23rd February, 1917. Pte. NICOLLS participated in the first attack on the morning of the 21st when he displayed great bravery in the face of hostile bombing. He was twice wounded, but refused to leave his post. In the second assault he was forging ahead with great dash when severely wounded by a grenade. He set a splendid example throughout.

2917 Private NIELSEN, Hans Kristian August, M.M.

M.M.—For conspicuous bravery and devotion to duty during a heavy bombardment of our trenches near GUEUDECOURT on the afternoon of 22/2/'17. Pte. NIELSEN showed great gallantry in tending wounded and removing them to cover. Later he worked without respite until thoroughly exhausted, carrying the wounded through heavy knee deep mud, being all the time under shell fire.

548 Sergeant O'DONNELL, John Roy, D.C.M.

D.C.M.—At POZIERES. On the evening of 5th August, Sgt. O'DONNELL was in charge of a platoon, and was taking his men up to the firing line. They had to pass through an intense artillery barrage, and as the sap was full of dead and wounded men, and seeing that his men showed signs of getting out of hand, he got them out of the sap and across the open country direct to the firing line. On arrival there he was of great assistance helping to consolidate and hold the line, showing exceptional bravery and coolness under trying circumstances.

3006 Private OLIVER, William Charles, D.C.M.

D.C.M.—For his marked initiative and courage whilst in the outpost line near DERNANCOURT, South West of ALBERT on March

31st, 1918. At dusk an enemy post was seen moving into position. Pte. OLIVER awaited his opportunity, and when he saw a good target offer he ripped out with his Lewis Gun, saw some men fall and others retreat. He immediately jumped out of trench and ran forward to investigate, capturing one light machine gun and a British Lewis Gun and found four dead Germans. He obtained assistance and brought back the guns and identifications. This man throughout the tour frequently showed devotion to duty and utter disregard for danger.

3873 Sergeant OLSEN, Oscar Volney, D.C.M. (M.I.D.).
D.C.M.—For conspicuous gallantry and devotion to duty during the attack West of BELLENGLISE on 18th September, 1918. He was fired on from a strong enemy position, but rushed it with a few men. He reached the position first and 24 of the enemy surrendered to him. He set his platoon a splendid example during the whole advance.

Lieut. O'REILLY, Peter Dominic, M.M.
M.M.—For bravery in the Field and devotion to duty.

2266 Private PAGE, William Frederick, M.M.
M.M.—For bravery and devotion to duty at Front Line trenches MOLENAARELSTHOEK on the 29th September, 1917. Pte. PAGE was a member of a Lewis Gun team in an advanced post. During some heavy hostile shelling a shell exploded in the post killing the No. 1 of the gun and wounding the remainder of the crew. Pte. PAGE in spite of only having the use of one arm, being severely wounded in the other, brought his gun back to the main line and notified the officer in charge of what had happened and was instrumental in having the rest of the wounded men brought in.

Major PARKER, Keith Shelly, M.C.
M.C.—For conspicuous gallantry and devotion to duty. He went forward under heavy artillery and machine gun fire, and established his aid post in a shell-hole, where he worked under most adverse conditions for five days without rest, attending the wounded of many units. He was under shell fire the whole time, and set a splendid example of devotion to duty.

Lieut. PARSONS, Frederick Ernest, M.C.
M.C.—For marked courage and determined leadership during the attack West of BELLENGLISE, on 18th September, 1918. He led his company through heavy enemy barrage, and dealt with several nests of machine guns, killing or capturing the crews and taking the guns. The right flank having become dangerously exposed, he led his reserve platoon against the enemy, who were massing there for a counter-attack, and took 120 prisoners and captured several machine guns.

4572 L'Cpl. PATTERSON, William Joseph, M.M.
M.M.—For courage and devotion to duty at ZONNEBEKE on night of 12/13th October, 1917, during enemy counter-attack. When all other means of communication had broken down and all other Company runners had become casualties he made several trips from Coy. H.Q. to Battn. H.Q. with important messages through a very severe enemy artillery and M.G. fire. The work performed by this runner was most valuable and enabled the Battn. Commander to keep in touch with the situation.

2222 Private PERKINS, Herbert George, M.M.
M.M.—For bravery in the Field and devotion to duty.

Lieut. Col. PERRY, Stanley Llewellyn, D.S.O., M.C. (M.I.D.)
M.C.—Near POZIERES. For conspicuous bravery and coolness shown during a heavy bombardment of our trenches on the 4th August, 1916. The portion of the trenches occupied by Capt. PERRY'S Coy. were being subjected to a very heavy fire both oblique and frontal, and casualties were heavy. At the commencement of bombardment, Capt. PERRY moved up into the front line of trenches and remained there until severely wounded. This is only one of the instances during the operations 5/14th August,

in which Capt. PERRY proved himself a most brave and capable Officer.

Hon Capt. PICKUP, Robert Samuel, M.C.

M.C.—for conspicuous gallantry and devotion to duty in action near DERNANCOURT, South West of ALBERT on 5th April, 1918. During the afternoon the enemy out in extremely heavy barrage down on one of our isolated trenches causing many casualties. Lieut. PICKUP crossed the open under very heavy fire and by his personal example and determined action succeeded in restoring order and confidence at the end of a very trying and exhausting day. He then returned under the same fire to his own post.

2671 T/Cpl. PORRITT, Alexander, M.M.

M.M.—For conspicuous bravery in an attack on an enemy strong point and trenches at GUEUDECOURT on the morning of 21/2/17. He led his section with great dash, and in the bombing operations along the trench set a splendid example of courage and leadership. He continued in the forefront of the party until severely wounded. His fine management of the bombing section contributed materially to the rapid progress of the whole party along the German trench.

Lieut. POTTS, Clarence McIntosh, M.C.

M.C.—For conspicuous gallantry and devotion to duty during operations East of HAMEL, from 8th to 11th August, 1918. He commanded his Company throughout the operation with such skill and dash that he secured his objective at little cost, capturing over 150 prisoners and a battery of 5.9 inch guns. On the morning of 9th August, he led a daylight patrol over 1000 yards from our lines thereby securing valuable information. The same evening he advanced our line about 2000 yards, his Company digging in under heavy machine gun fire. Always cool and confident he set a fine example to his Company.

3988 Private PRINCE, Henry Russell, M.M.

M.M.—On the night of 15/16th October, 1916, during a raid on the German trenches near DIEPENDAAL. He was a signaller in charge of the telephone taken out into NO MAN'S LAND and displayed coolness and courage in his efforts to keep up communication.

3449 Corporal RITCHIE, Arthur Ford, M.M.

M.M.—For bravery and devotion to duty during the operations near DERNANCOURT, South West of ALBERT, from 1st-5th April, 1918. He displayed extraordinary coolness and gallant leadership. Going through a barrage on the morning of 5th April, 1918, when his men became disorganised he rallied them and led them cheering them up by singing ragtime songs. On the morning of 3rd April, 1918, he stood up in full view of the enemy and directed trench mortar fire on a number of Germans who were moving towards our line. This was done amidst a hail of M.G. bullets.

4065 Corporal ROBERTS, Hugh, M.M.

M.M.—Stretcher Bearer, for coolness and devotion to duty shown by him on the 23rd November, 1916, while carrying a wounded man from GREASE TRENCH, near GUEUDECOURT to the support trench. Owing to there being no communication trench the wounded had to be carried overland and on this occasion the sniping was bad. Though wounded by a sniper he stuck to his job and succeeded in getting the wounded man back to the support trench.

2019 Private SADLER, James Rudolph, M.M.

M.M.—For conspicuous gallantry and devotion to duty during operations East of HAMEL, East of CORBIE, from 8th to 11th August, 1918. This soldier is a stretcher bearer and on the morning of the 10th when one of our posts was severely shelled and several casualties sustained this soldier with utter disregard for personal safety went out and dressed the wounded, and afterwards brought them in. He undoubtedly saved the lives of men wounded. His courage was at all times beyond all praise.

Captain SCHADEL, William Herbert, M.C.

M.C.—For conspicuous gallantry and devotion to duty. When his post was attacked by a party of twenty enemy with a machine gun, he went forward with a strong patrol at a critical moment, succeeded in driving them off, and captured their gun. It was due to his quick appreciation of the situation and swift action that the attack was repulsed and the post remained intact.

Lieut. SCOTT, Reynold John, D.C.M.

D.C.M.—For exceptional bravery and devotion to duty in leading a team of bombers in an attack on the enemy's trenches at GUEUDECOURT on the night of 22/23rd. Feb., 1917. The assault was delivered under cover of Stokes Gun barrage. Watching the lift of the barrage Sgt. SCOTT dashed forward with his team and successfully bombed the Germans out. He then assisted to organise the rifle grenadiers and was of great assistance in keeping the Germans at a distance until the block was erected and the position consolidated. Sgt. SCOTT also displayed great daring in the preliminary reconnaisance and the work done in this respect proved to be of great value in the subsequent attack.

3119 Corporal SECOMB, Claude Leslie, M.M.

M.M.—For conspicuous gallantry in an attack on enemy strong point, and trenches at GUEUDECOURT on the morning of 21/2/'17. He was always to the fore in a hand-to-hand encounter along the trench and was one of the first party whose splendid dash and determination overcame all opposition. When the trench was captured he remained at the block and gave great assistance in repelling an enemy counter-attack.

2484 Corporal SELLICK, Frederick George, D.C.M.

D.C.M.—For conspicuous gallantry and devotion to duty during the operations East of HAMEL from 8th to 11th August, 1918. This soldier is a Battalion Scout and during the advance was ahead of the attacking troops looking for machine gun nests and posts. When he discovered these he used his light Lewis Gun with great effect, inflicting casualties on them and keeping their heads down until they were rushed by the oncoming troops, and in this manner prevented casualties in the advancing lines. Later during a minor operation he was a member of a fighting patrol which brought back valuable information. At all times bold and courageous, he set a magnificent example to all.

Lieut. SIMPSON, George Alfred, M.M.

M.M.—North West of POZIERES. On the night of 6/7th August, 1916, there was a heavy hostile artillery barrage between battalion headquarters and the firing line, and the wire was cut on several occasions. Sgt. SIMPSON was out the whole night repairing breaks and showed exceptional bravery and coolness under very dangerous and trying conditions.

4527 Sergeant SIMPSON, George Henty, M.M.

M.M.—At POZIERES on the night 7/8th August, 1916, Pte. SIMPSON was carrying out his duties as runner between the firing line and the support line. There was a heavy hostile artillery fire all night and although Pte. SIMPSON was hit early in the evening, he never reported himself as wounded until the next morning having carried messages all night.

4477 Sergeant SMITH, Charles, D.C.M.

D.C.M.—For conspicuous gallantry and devotion to duty during the operations West of BELLENGLISE on 18th September, 1918. At one time during the advance our Right Flank was dangerously exposed owing to the troops on our right being held up by a strong detachment of the enemy. Sgt. SMITH, who was in charge of the right half platoon, with great skill and determination, manoeuvred his command in such a manner that he was able to engage the enemy at short range and force him to evacuate, our line being thereby established. This N.C.O. set a splendid example to the men throughout.

Captain SORRELL, John Harold Ashley, **M.M.**

M.M.—For gallantry shown on the 21st August, 1915. He was then a stretcher bearer in the 13th Battn., A.I.F., and showed exceptional bravery in bringing in wounded men under heavy rifle and machine gun fire.

5186 Private STEEL, William, **M.M.**

M.M.—At BULLECOURT on 11th April, 1917, as a runner this soldier displayed great bravery in delivering a despatch from the HINDENBURG Line to the 12th M.G. Coy Headquarters at NORIEUL. He passed through heavy artillery and machine gun fire and although badly wounded in the head he delivered his despatch before evacuated to hospital.

2/Lieut. STEVENS, Albert Edward, **M.M.**

M.M.—For consistent good work in the firing line at POZIERES from the night of August 5th until the morning of August 8th, 1916. During most of that time the trenches were subjected to a very heavy bombardment. Sgt. STEVENS was acting as platoon commander and his courage and fearlessness was instrumental in helping to keep the garrison of the trench in good spirits and also greatly assisted his Company Commander.

4479 Private STOREY, Robert, **M.M.**

M.M.—For exceptional courage in an attack on enemy strong point and trench at GUEUDECOURT on the morning of 21/2/'17. After the capture of the enemy strong point he continued to bomb along the trench in the face of the enemy opposition and most exhausting conditions. The mud was thigh deep, but he forged ahead until the objective was obtained. He then worked energetically in the erection of a block and showed great spirit during the repulse of a German counter-attack.

2494 L/Cpl. Driver THORNLEY, Albert Ernest, **M.M.**

M.M.—For conspicuous gallantry and devotion to duty during the advance West of BELLENGLISE on 18/9/'18. The Driver volunteered the Battalion Mule Train. In spite of a heavy enemy barrage which fell in the area through which they had to pass and also a dense fog which made maintenance of direction extremely hard, the mules arrived in good time. Two of the mules became casualties and their load had to be dumped. After delivering his load this man returned through the barrage and assisted to bring the remainder to the appointed destination. It was due to his brave conduct and perseverance that supplies were brought forward when most required.

3159 T/Sgt. THURECHT, Norman David, **M.M.**

M.M.—For conspicuous gallantry and devotion to duty during the attack West of BELLENGLISE on the 18/9/'18. After being wounded he remained on duty and led his section through a very heavy enemy barrage. Despite his wound he showed admirable coolness and courage and refused to remain behind, but continued in the advance encouraging and rallying his men until wounded the second time.

2726 Private TOFT, Arthur Stanley, **M.M.**

M.M.—During the operations East of HAMEL, East of CORBIE on the 8/8/'18 this soldier, a member of a mopping up party in CAROLINE WOOD, whilst clearing several dugouts he was fired on from one of them. At great risk he rushed this dugout, killed two of the occupants and took the remaining 6 prisoners. This soldier has always done good work and his courage and coolness are remarkable.

3253 Corporal TOZER, Walter Charles, **M.M.**

M.M.—For his gallant conduct and prompt action at VILLERS BRETONNEUX East of AMIENS on the 2nd May, 1918. At about 5 a.m. a party of Germans were advancing on his post which was in an isolated position having just been established and which it was of the utmost importance to hold. He immediately opened fire on the party with his Lewis Gun causing a number of casualties. It was due to his very prompt action that the attack was delayed and finally driven off. His work during the whole tour in the line was excellent.

4900 Private TURNER, Arthur, M.M.

M.M.—For conspicuous gallantry and devotion to duty. During the minor operations of the 7/8th July, near HAMEL, East of CORBIE this soldier was a member of a squad to wire the new position. At 12.20 a.m. the enemy put down a heavy artillery barrage and this man was wounded in the shoulder and when ordered to the rear persisted in collecting his rifle and equipment. His conduct was inspiring and a great example to his platoon.

1410 Corporal TURNER, Gilbert, M.M.

M.M.—For bravery and devotion to duty during an attack on an enemy trench North East of GUEUDECOURT on the night of 22/23rd February, 1917, also during the afternoon of 22nd Feby., when it was very essential that communication be kept up in view of the attack that night. He went out on three separate occasions notwithstanding a heavy artillery barrage and fixed up breaks in the wire between the front line and Battalion Headquarters also while the attack was in progress he was out practically continuously repairing wires. By his coolness under fire and promptitude of action his work generally was most valuable.

4902 Private TURVEY, Thomas Henry, M.M.

M.M.—For his gallant conduct and devotion to duty during an attack on an enemy trench near GUEDECOURT on the night of 22/23rd Feb., 1917. When as a runner he maintained a communication overland under artillery and machine gun fire between the front line and Headquarters. His work in this respect was quite consistent with his previous fine record established for coolness and determination in the face of all obstacles.

572 W.O. TUSON, Ernest Vernon, M.C., M.M. (M.I.D.)

M.C.—For consistent good work and devotion to duty during the period 26th February to 20th September, 1917. The example set and work done by R.S.M. TUSON both during operations and when the Battalion has been training, has been of an exceptionally high standard. Has been awarded Military Medal.

572 W.O. TUSON, Ernest Vernon, M.C., M.M. (M.I.D.)

M.M.—For exceptional bravery and coolness shown by him on the night of 2nd and 3rd May, 1915, when serving as a Corporal in "D" Coy., 13th Bn., A.I.F. The Battalion was taking part in a night attack on that date, when, coming under heavy fire and it being impossible to advance further, orders were given to dig in and hold on. The platoon commander and Sgt. being both wounded Cpl. TUSON took the platoon in hand and was instrumental in holding an important part of the line.

3948 Corporal VENABLES, Cecil Herbert, M.M.

M.M.—On the night of 15/16th October, 1916, during a raid on the German trenches near DIEPENDAAL He was in charge of a bombing section and displayed coolness and courage. Owing to being delayed by hostile fire, the only other member of his section to enter a hostile trench with him was Pte. CLARK, but without delay or hesitation they carried out the work detailed for the section to do.

3038 Private VERRALL, Frank Henry, M.M.

M.M.—For conspicuous gallantry and devotion to duty during the operation East of HAMEL, East of CORBIE, from 8th to 11th August, 1918. This soldier was in the leading section of his platoon which was being fired on by the enemy from a small wood. Without hesitation he dashed ahead and successfully dealt with 2 Officers and 6 men. Throughout the operation he set a magnificent example of courage, initiative and determination.

Lieut. VINCENT, James, M.C. and Bar., D.C.M. (M.I.D.)

For his excellent work and untiring energy in obtaining intelligence and information and carrying out his duty as Scout Officer at DERNANCOURT, South West of ALBERT, on April

5th, 1918. With great foresight and sound judgment he chose the sight for the Battalion to dig in during a very heavy barrage and gave invaluable assistance to Coy. Commanders in helping to get the Companies into position. When the Battalion moved forward to the position preparing to attack on 5th April, 1918, Lieut. VINCENT, with his knowledge of the ground gained by previous reconnaisances under very heavy fire was again able to be of great assistance to the Coy. Commanders in preparing the line of attack. Time after time he went forward through a terrific barrage of M.G. fire to the line and brought back valuable information to Battalion H. Qrs. Through his ability in quickly sizing up the situation and his keenness in obtaining any information which would be useful he kept Battalion H.Qrs. posted in every move of the companies and the general situation.

Lieut. VINCENT, James, M.C. and Bar., D.C.M. (M.I.D.)
Bar to M.C.—For conspicuous gallantry and devotion to duty during an attack. In very thick fog he went forward and successfully laid the tape on the battalion jumping-off line, which was 2 miles away. He then guided the tanks into position, and during the advance he preceded the battalion with his scouts, spraying enemy positions with three light Lewis guns, and at one point cutting off the retreat of about 100 of the enemy. He set a splendid example of cool courage and determination.

Lieut. VINCENT, James, M.C. and Bar., D.C.M. (M.I.D.)
D.C.M.—For conspicuous gallantry and devotion to duty on several occasions. He continually stimulated his company by his coolness and courage under heavy fire, showing great ability and initiative in consolidating a captured position and leading a patrol into enemy country and gaining most valuable information.

2696 L/Cpl. WADE, William George, M.M.
M.M.—For conspicuous courage at ZONNEBEKE on the 12th October, 1917. He guided numerous parties up to the jumping-off position preparatory to attack and during a very heavy enemy barrage which followed, and though wounded, he continued in the execution of his duties in guiding up carrying parties to the most forward positions. His determination to carry out his duties though wounded set a fine example to all.

2452 Sergeant WALKER, Robert Allan, M.M.
M.M.—for bravery and coolness on the night 29/30th August, 1916, at POZIERES. When owing to a heavy hostile artillery barrage the wire connecting the firing line and Battalion Headquarters was continually being cut. L/Cpl. WALKER was out practically the whole night repairing the wire, and notwithstanding the dangerous and trying conditions, succeeded in keeping up communications.

3972 Sergeant WALLACE, Eric John, M.M.
M.M.—For conspicuous gallantry and devotion to duty during the operations East of HAMEL from 8/11/8/'18. This N.C.O. was in charge of a mopping-up party. He cleared dugouts and artillery emplacements capturing many prisoners and much material. Whilst ably directing the consolidation of his platoon on the objective he was seriously wounded.

3736 Private WALLACE, Joseph, M.M.
M.M.—For conspicuous gallantry and devotion to duty during the operations East of CORBIE from 8th to 11th August, 1918. During the attack he rushed a machine gun post which was enfilading his platoon, capturing the gun and crew single-handed.

3737 Private WALLACE, Robert Gordon, M.M.
M.M.—For conspicuous gallantry and devotion to duty during operations East of HAMEL from 8/11/8/'18. This soldier was in charge of his section throughout the operations. At one point he was fired on by an enemy machine gun. He immediately worked round and reached the gun from the rear, thereby capturing the gun and crew.

Lieut. WATT, James, M.M.

M.M.—On the night 15/16th October, 1916, during a raid on the German trenches near DIEPENDAAL. He was in charge of the covering party in NO MAN'S LAND and carried out his work under difficult conditions, with judgment and coolness.

2746 L/Cpl. WEBBER, George, M.M.

M.M.—For conspicuous bravery and endurance at ZONNEBEKE on 12th October, 1917, during heavy enemy barrage and counter-attack. He went out into NO MAN'S LAND several times and bandaged and carried wounded men back to our lines, thus saving many of his comrades. His coolness and courage was most marked and was an example to all.

3950 Private WELSH, John, M.M.

M.M.—For conspicuous gallantry during our bombing attack on MUNSTER ALLEY South of BAPAUME ROAD on 7th August, 1916, in that he covered the party, building a block near the head of the trench.

448 Sergeant WHEAL, Frank, M.M.

M.M.—For conspicuous courage and devotion to duty near HAMEL, East of CORBIE, on night 30th June/1st July, 1918. He was a volunteer for a patrol with his platoon Commander to secure a Hun. An enemy working party of 30 having been located about 700 yards from our lines, he, with his platoon Commander, rushed the nearest one and took him prisoner. Afterwards this N.C.O. covered the withdrawal, and although the enemy rallied he was beaten off with loss and the party returned to our lines without a casualty. He displayed the greatest courage and coolness throughout a daring operation.

3496 Corporal WHITE, Rupert James, M.M.

M.M.—For conspicuous gallantry and devotion to duty during the attack near DERNANCOURT RIDGE, South West of ALBERT, on 5th April, 1918. When his Officer was killed and all other N.C.O.'s were out of action he took charge of the platoon rallied his men and led them to the attack. Although wounded in the shoulder he carried on and consolidated his platoon position. At nightfall he, in company with L/Cpl. RITCHIE, went forward and located the position of the enemy so successfully and brought back such information as enabled his company commander to make his defensive position secure where it might have been weak.

2696 Private WICKERS, Walter Thomas, M.M.

M.M.—for bravery in the Field and devotion to duty.

2992 Sergeant WILLIAMS, William, D.C.M.

D.C.M.—For conspicuous gallantry and devotion to duty in attacking an enemy strong point that was holding up our attack, and capturing twenty-three prisoners, aided by four of his comrades. He personally reconnoitred the trenches round the strong point, and gained valuable information, afterwards assisting very ably to break up a hostile counter-attack.

3549 L/Cpl. WILLIS, Henry Peter, M.M.

M.M.—For bravery in the Field and devotion to duty.

796 C.S.M. WISE, James Peel, M.S.M.

M.S.M.—For distinguished conduct and devotion to duty in the field. Since leaving Australia in 1914 this W.O. has displayed consistent coolness and gallantry in action, coupled with ability to lead men and set them a praiseworthy example of endurance under the hardships and dangers of Active Service. As C.S.M. he has been of great value to his company both in and out of the line from September, 1917, to February, 1918. He has been brought to notice for distinguished conduct in every action of his battalion in France.

2740 Private WITTON, Geoffrey Forbes, M.M.

M.M.—For conspicuous courage and devotion to duty during the attack West of BELLENGLISE on the 18/9/'18, when his Battalion passed through a very heavy enemy barrage. This man was acting as stretcher bearer and although carrying a large quantity of extra supplies he was particularly assiduous in dressing and attending the wounded. He remained in the barrage whilst there were any wounded to attend to, and throughout displayed admirable courage and cheerfulness.

4346 Corporal WORNER, Walter John, M.M.

M.M.—For splendid dash and determination in an attack on enemy strong point and trenches at GUEUDECOURT on the morning of 21/2/'17. When sent forward to reinforce he forged through almost impassable mud which was being subjected to a hail of enemy grenades. He took the position of first bayonet man and acted with great determination. He also showed skill in the effective use of rifle grenades which were employed with great success.

800 L/Cpl. YOUNG, Hughie Edward, M.M.

M.M.—At POZIERES. Pte. YOUNG, a stretcher bearer, attached to "C" Coy., worked continuously carrying wounded from the front line to the dressing station from the evening of the 5th August until he was himself wounded (while attending to a wounded man) on the night of 7/8th August, 1916. While making his trips he frequently had to pass through heavy artillery barrages, and furthermore to move over open country, as the saps were too narrow for stretchers.

Lieut. YOUNG, James, M.C., D.C.M. (M.I.D.)

D.C.M.—For bravery and coolness under very dangerous and trying circumstances on the afternoon of the 14/8/'16 while on duty in the front line at POZIERES. The trench was being heavily bombarded at the time and the explosion of one shell partly buried the company commander (Capt. PERRY) and half a dozen other ranks. Although badly shaken C.S.M. YOUNG assisted to dig out Capt. PERRY and sent him to the rear (severly wounded and unconscious) and then set to work superintending the repairing of the trench until another company commander relieved him. This is only one of several occasions C.S.M. YOUNG proved himself a very cool and capable N.C.O. when conditions were both trying and dangerous.

Lieut. YOUNG, James, M.C., D.C.M. (M.I.D.)

M.C.—For coolness, courage and leadership at DERNANCOURT, South West of ALBERT, on April 1st, 1918. After the hurricane bombardment of DERNANCOURT on Afternoon of April 1st, Lieut. YOUNG was sent to patrol the village. On reaching outskirts 2 M.G.'s opened up 15 yards to his right and his patrol halted by a post immediately in front, thus cutting him off and forcing him into a tight corner. This Officer immediately displayed his usual leadership and initiative by despatching a section to deal with the guns and himself led an assault on the guns post forcing them to beat a hasty retreat. The advance was pushed to the road where the patrol was met by a superior force. With great coolness Lieut. YOUNG organised the withdrawal which was completed after giving assistance to the section dealing with the M.G.'s without casualties. His devotion to duty and work up to the time he was wounded in the attack on April 5th, 1918, was exemplary.

Capt. YOUNG, William Lancelot, M.C. (M.I.D.)

M.C.—For gallantry in leading a raid into enemy's trenches near DIEPENDAAL on the night 15/16th October, 1916. Capt. YOUNG carefully organised and trained this raiding party, handled it very skilfully when the raid entered the enemy trenches, and subsequently withdrew, bringing four wounded men away with him. This officer also distinguished himself at POZIERES on 5th to 7th August, when he commanded a Company with conspicuous ability.

APPENDIX III.

OFFICIAL NOMINAL ROLL OF THE BATTALION.

2857 Abbott, A. C., Pte.
5326 Abbott, A. J., Pte.
3226 Abbott, G. T., Pte.
3262 Abel, L. W., Pte.
Abel, S. J., Capt.
3231 Abrahams, J. T., Pte.
3103 Abrahams, M., Pte.
3594 Acland, R. E., Pte.
2126 Adam, W. T., Pte.
7681 Adams, E. R., Pte.
3592 Adams, J. C., Pte.
3001 Adams, M., Pte.
1311 Adams, P., Corp.
2551 Adams, R., Pte.
Adams, W. G., Capt., D.S.O., M.C. (M.I.D.)
2373 Affleck, A. J., Sergt. M.M.
2068 Agar, W. A., Corp.
7683 Agnew, C. H., Corp.
2781 Agst, D. A., Pte.
2371 Aitchison, T., Pte.
4648 Akin, T. J., Dvr.
1059 Alabaster, W., Sergt., M.M.
4336 Alchin, A. F., Pte.
4490 Alexander, B. H., Sapper.
2280 Alexander, T. J., Pte.
2555 Alford, E. S., Pte.
3276 Allen, L., Pte. (stated to be B. L.)
2383 Allan, W. D. G., Pte.
Allen, A. S., Lieut. Col., D.S.O., C. de G. French (M.I.D.)
4052 Allen, H., Pte.
Allen, H. B., Lieut.
Allen, J. H. Lieut.
14915 Allen, R. T., Pte.
2372 Allen, T., Pte.
2124 Allen, W. F., Pte.
2127 Allen, W. G., Pte.
2860 Allen, W. R., Pte.
1303 Allen, W. T., Pte.
1615 Allison, I., Corp.
Allman, J. T., Lieut. M.M.
3506 Allner, J. J., Pte.
3104 Allport, C. E. L/Cpl.
3226 Allright, W. A., Pte.
2344 Ambler, R. G., Corp.
587 Amer, J., Sergt.
5594 Ames, C., Dvr.
3349 Amies, A. L., Pte.
3395 Anderson, H. T., Pte.
1677 Anderson, J. D., Corp.
Anderson, J. R., Capt. M.C.

3101 Anderson, M. J., T/Dvr.
4546 Anderson, R. C., Pte.
4548 Anderson, W. H., Pte.
5130 Andrew, A. W., Pte.
4433 Andrews, B., Pte.
2122 Angus, E., Pte.
2861 Angus, W. G., Pte.
4726 Anlezark, L. R., Pte.
2123 Annan, F. C., L/Cpl. M.M.
3229 Ansell, T., Pte., M.M.
3502 Anson, F. G., Sap. (Stated to be Anson-de-Vincer, F. G.)
3348 Anson, R. A., Sap.
2370 Anthony, J. G., Pte.
4426 Apsley, W., Pte.
7194 Arbuckle, A., ER/2/ Cpl.
1669 Archer, C., Pte.
2368 Archer, S. J., Pte.
3001 Archibald, A. H., Dvr.
3275 Archibald, R. C. W., Pte.
4128 Archibald, R. H., Pte.
3598 Arman, J., Pte.
Armson, S., Chap.
1867 Armstrong, C. R., Pte.
1866 Armstrong, E. E., Pte.
3681 Armstrong, L., Bombdr.
2859 Armstrong, R. G., Pte.
1666 Arndale, E. L., Pte.
3882 Arnold, C., Dvr.
1868 Arnold, E. H., Pte.
2367 Arnold, T. W., Pte.
2121 Artery, W. A., Pte.
1668 Arthur, R. C., L/Cpl.
3350 Asbrey, C. F., Pte.
2366 Ash, R. J., Pte.
3524 Ashman, A. J., Pte.
1869 Ashwell, J. R., Pte.
2611 Askew, F., A/Sgt.
1309 Aslatt, H. F., Sergt. D.C.M., M.M., M.S.M.
3597 Astridge, A., Pte.
2856 Atkins, A., Pte.
2369 Atkinson, E. R., Corp.
2113 Atkinson, T. H., Pte.
3981 Attenborough, M., Bombdr.
2125 Aubrey, J. C., Pte.
2105 Austin, F., Pte., M.M.

4726 Austin, H. B., Pte.
3102 Auswild, G. A., Pte.
467 Avery, H., Pte.
5328 Aylett, W., Pte.
4432 Aylin, A. E., Pte.
1875 Aylward, T. W., Sergt.
5034 Ayres, F. A., Pte.
2120 Baalman, J., Sergt.
2815 Babinett, J. T., Pte.
3612 Backhouse, G., Pte.
2870 Backhouse, J., Pte.
3109 Backhouse, R. J., Pte.
1703 Bacon, F. M., Pte.
1616 Bagnall, W. F., Sap.
4553 Bagust, H. A., Dvr.
2869 Bahn, J., Pte.
4488 Bailey, A. E. H., Sergt., M.M.
807 Bailey, A. R., Dvr.
3265 Bailey, C. E., Pte.
4489 Bailey, E. L., C.S.M. M.M.
7028 Bailey, F. J., Pte.
2789 Bailey, P. R., Bomdr.
706 Bailey, W. C., C.S.M.
3114 Bain, A. T., L/Cpl.
2867 Bain, W. H., Pte. (Stated to be Anderson, William George.)
5048 Baird, B. S., Pte.
1888 Baker, C. N., Pte.
2778 Baker, G. A., Pte.
2619 Baker, G. C., Pte.
4487 Baker, G. W., Corp.
Baker, H., Lieut.
2622 Baker, H. E., Pte.
2872 Baker, L. F., Pte.
1650 Baker, S., Pte.
3355 Baker, S. E., Pte.
2612 Baker, T., Pte.
2723 Baker, V. R., ER/2/Cpl.
3488 Baker, W. G., Pte.
4731 Baker, W. R., L/Cpl.
123 Baker, W. W., Pte.
2140 Balderston, D. P., Pte.
1872 Baldwin, C. H., Pte.
2868 Baldwin, T., Pte.
3010 Balfour, A. St. G., Pte.
7455 Ball, J., Pte.
4556 Ballard, M. H., Corp.
7027 Ballenden, J. G., Pte.
4682 Bampton, C. E., Pte.
3506 Banks, R., Pte.
1912 Bannister, W. J., Corp., D.C.M.
Barber, C., Lieut., M.M.

6671 Burrowes, J. L., Pte.
3993 Burrows, R. G., Dvr.
4560 Burton, A., Dvr.
3018 Burton, A. W., Pte.
2137 Burton, S. A., Pte.
3610 Bush, J. W., Pte.
4152 Bushell, R. W., Pte.
M.M.
7694 Bussell, O., Pte.
3024 Butler, A., Pte.
1604 Butler, A. E., Corp.
54387 Butler, G. F., Pte.
2383 Butler, W. G., Pte.
1870 Butt, J. H., Pte.
54386 Butt, R. H., Pte.
2345 Butt, W., Sapper.
1510 Butterworth, R., Sergt.
3614 Buttle, W., Pte.
3701 Button, W., Pte.
3115 Byass, T. L., Pte.
5050 Byers, W. R., Pte.
4460 Byrnes, J., Pte.
2518 Byrnes, P. J. J., Pte.
2031 Byrnes, R., Pte.
1721 Bywater, E., Pte.
7721 Caddey, W., Pte.
3126 Caesar, A. J., L/Cpl.
2368 Caffery, J. J., Pte.
1742 Caffrey, L., Pte.
3127 Cain, E., Pte.
13158 Cairnduff, R. P., Corp.
3724 Cairns, A. E., L/Cpl.
3741 Calder, D., Pte.
7711 Caldwell, A. E., T/Sgt.
2570 Callaghan, H., Pte.
3622 Callaway, E., ER/2/Cpl.
3714 Calley, F. A., Pte.
467 Calman, J. C., Pte.
243 Calvert, T., Corp.
3743 Cambridge, K. R., Pte.
Cameron, D., 2/Lt.
2881 Cameron, I. C., Pte.
4747 Cameron, J. G., C.S.M., D.C.M.
2885 Cameron, R. S., Pte.
3528 Campbell, A. C., Pte.
1893 Campbell, A. St. C., Pte.
2270 Campbell, D. C., Pte.
2391 Campbell, G., Pte.
2155 Campbell, H. W., Pte.
2893 Campbell, K. D., Corp.
5669 Campling, G. W., L/Cpl.
2874 Campman, C., Pte.
4168 Cantle, C., Pte.
3716 Cantrill, S. W., Pte.
7710 Cantwell, J. P., Pte.
7048 Cantwell, M. J., Pte.

3359 Canty, A. J., Pte.
3723 Canvin, J. R., Pte.
2757 Capon, M., Pte.
2625 Cardell, G. P. F., R/Sgt.
2884 Cardwell, G. S., Pte.
3736 Carew, F., Pte.
3734 Carey, J., L/Cpl.
1332 Carey, R., Pte.
3033 Carmichael, W. H., L/Sgt.
2143 Carne, H. H., Pte.
3276 Carnegie, A. E., Pte.
2248 Carr, C., Pte.
2756 Carr, J. W., L/Cpl.
3364 Carr, J. W., Pte.
2393 Carr, W., Pte.
7349 Carroll, C. P., Pte.
1985 Carroll, L. T., Sergt.
2471 Carroll, R. G., Pte.
2159 Carroll, R. W., Pte.
3288 Carroll, V., Pte.
2158 Carroll, W. C., Pte.
2802 Carroll, W. H., Pte.
(Stated to be Jury, Evered William Hope.)
1045 Carruthers, W., Dvr.
4155 Carson, J., Pte.
5353 Carter, E. C., Pte.
2314 Carter, G. H., Pte.
3624 Carter, H., Pte.
5069 Carter, H., Pte.
3480 Carter, I. A., Pte.
2631 Carter, N. W., Pte.
4377 Carter, P. E., Pte.
3623 Cartwright, A. G., Pte.
7870 Cartwright, F., Pte.
7175 Cartwright, H. G., Pte.
4745 Carver, S. R., Sergt.
1644 Casey, P., Pte.
1741 Casey, P., L/Cpl. M.M.
1890 Cassell, G. W., L/Sgt., M.M.
1891 Cassell, L., Pte.
4156 Cassidy, J., Pte.
3621 Cassin, J., Pte.
3350 Catchpoole, W. H., R., L/Cpl.
2886 Cathro, C. B., Pte.
4017 Caughey, J., L/Cpl. M.M.
3123 Chadwick, P. A., Dvr.
1516 Chalk, W. R., Pte.
4922 Chalker, E. E., Pte.
4157 Chalker, H. J., Pte.
1894 Chalmers, A. M., Pte.
3039 Chalmers, J., Pte.
5355 Chamberlain, T., Corp., M.M.
2576 Chambers, F. H., Pte.

3266 Chambers, W. J., Pte.
3740 Channells, R. C., Pte.
4494 Chant, J. E., Gun.
2388 Chapman, A. H., Dvr.
3618 Chapman, B., Pte.
Chapman, D., Major.
715 Chapman, H. L., Pte.
4758 Chapman, J., L/Cpl.
2887 Chapman, J. V., T/Cpl.
2892 Chapman, W. H., Pte.
3719 Chappell, W., Pte.
4023 Chapple, R. S., Pte.
3717 Chard, C. P., Pte.
3774 Chargois, V. H., Pte.
3015 Charles, W., Pte.
349 Charlton, W. H., Pte.
2298 Charman, C. A., Pte.
2147 Cheesman, R. H., Pte.
7715 Cheetham, H. T., Pte.
4167 Chenail, E. M. R., Pte.
3619 Chester, H. H., Pte.
3125 Chettle, W. T., Pte.
Chew, A. N., Lieut. C de G., Belgian, (M.I.D.)
2962 Chiene, F. C., Pte.
1714 Chisholm, D. S., C.S.M.
1895 Chittenden, G. C., Pte.
54399 Chivas, W., Pte.
2389 Christensen, J. A. A., Pte.
5752 Christie, E., Pte. Alias Wills, Albert.)
1692 Christie, M., Pte.
5359 Churton, W., Pte.
3124 Clancey, J. M., Pte.
2150 Clancy, L. D., Sergt.
2477 Clare, T. W., Sergt. M.M.
1895 Clark, G., Pte.
2876 Clark, J., Pte.
2970 Clark, J. J., Pte.
2156 Clark, P. H., Pte.
7718 Clark, P. R., Pte.
1683 Clark, W. H., L/Cpl., M.M.
2807 Clarke, A. N., L/Cpl.
3042 Clarke, A. R. J., Pte., M.M.
Clark, G. H., Capt.
2157 Clarke, H. F., Pte.
5053 Clarke, J. C., Pte.
7709 Clarke, J. F., Pte.
2891 Clarke, S. B., Pte.
1928 Clarke, T. P., Sgt.
3122 Clarke, W., Pte.

2544 Clarke, W. M., Pte.
2770 Clarkson, M. T., Pte.
5360 Clarkson, W. H., Pte.
     Clayton, A., 2/Lieut.
3021 Clear, L. A, Pte.
2938 Clemence, J. E., Cpl.
 382 Clemo, W., Pte.
4756 Clement, W., Pte.
2633 Clemson, L. H., Pte.
2958 Clifton, R., Pte.
2634 Close, J. A., Pte.
3625 Close, R. A., Sap.
5350 Coates, T., L/Cpl.
1702 Cobcroft, R. H., Pte.
1901 Cochran, W. C., Pte.
2525 Cochrane, W. J., Pte.
4024 Coffey, P., Pte.
3360 Coffey, E. X., Pte.
2400 Cogan, E. V., Pte.
3583 Cohen, C. S., Pte.
3119 Colbert, S., Pte.
2572 Cole, H. J., Pte.
2573 Cole, R. T., Sgt.
1113 Coleborne, S. L., Pte.
2522 Coleman, J., Pte.
3722 Coleman, T. W., Pte.
1898 Coles, W. T., L/Cpl.
2973 Coll, P. J., T/C. S.M. (D.C.M., M.M.)
2580 Collen, H. J. W., Cpl.
3019 Collins, A. N,. Pte.
4748 Collins, C. J., Pte.
2523 Collins, R. H., Sap.
3746 Collins, S. J., Pte.
7725 Collins, T., Pte.
 484 Collins, W. G., Dvr.
5061 Collins, W. O., Pte.
3368 Collins, W. T., Pte.
3724 Collis, F. H., Cpl.
2152 Colliver, W., L/Cpl. M.M
 483 Collopy, C. R., Cpl.
1332 Collum, F. E., Sgt.
2634 Colwell, F. R., L/Cpl.
3737 Colyer, H. S., Pte.
1755 Comer, E. H., Pte.
2579 Comport, A., Pte.
2875 Compton, J., Pte.
4762 Condon, J., Pte.
1888 Condon, T. J., Pte.
7045 Condron, T. D., Pte.
2394 Conlin, W. G., Pte.
2160 Connell, F., Pte.
3742 Connellan, L. V. J., Dvr.
3362 Connelly, R. M., Pte.

3763 Connery, R. P., Pte.
1899 Connolly, P. O., Pte.
2627 Connolly, T. P., Pte.
1111 Connop, J. V., L/Cpl.
2149 Conroy, A. H., Cpl.
1743 Consadine, J. J., Pte.
1330 Considine, P. J., Sgt.
2629 Constable, R., Pte.
2146 Convey, W. H., Pte.
2392 Conway, J., Pte.
5101 Conwell, W. D., Pte.
2814 Cook, C., Pte.
2154 Cook, E. J. T., Pte.
1645 Cook, H., Pte.
3361 Cook, H., Pte.
2630 Cook, H. J., Pte.
2135 Cook, J., Pte.
2350 Cook, R., L/Cpl.
2628 Cook, R. F., Pte.
3617 Cook, R. E., Pte.
3121 Cook, T. J., Pte.
7713 Cook, W., Pte.
2878 Cook, W. A., Pte.
4355 Cooke, A., Pte.
3046 Cooke, H. E., Pte.
3294 Cooke, H. J., Sgt.
 143 Cooke, J. C., Cpl.
 984 Coombes, R. A., Sgt., M.M.
4565 Coombes, A., Pte.
7717 Cooper, C., Pte.
4013 Cooper, C. G., Pte.
15075 Cooper, E. S., Pte.
7723 Cooper, J. E., Pte.
4750 Cooper, P. F., L/Cpl.
5068 Cooper, T., Pte.
 144 Cooper, W. J., Gnr.
2809 Copland, B., Dvr.
4650 Copland, W., Gnr.
3709 Coram, F., Dvr.
3292 Corbett, J. J., Gnr.
     Corbett, L. R., Lieut.
3710 Corbishley, W. J., L/Cpl.
2524 Corin, W. B., Pte.
4020 Corkery, W. J., Dvr.
1681 Corliss, J. F., Pte.
4521 Corne, P., Pte.
4156 Cornish, E. J., Pte.
     Cornish, E. W., Capt., M.C. and Bar.
 361 Cornish, H., Sgt.
2533 Cornish, W. T., Gnr.
54403 Costello, E. A., Pte.
3700 Costello, H. C., Pte.
4666 Costello, J., Pte.
5349 Costello, M., Pte.

5072 Costello, M. C., Pte.
1662 Costello, T., Pte.
4165 Costin, R. H., Pte.
2571 Cotterill, J., Pte.
3278 Coughlin, M., Pte.
2151 Coull, S. A., Pte.
4743 Coutts, H. C, Pte.
     Coward, H. K., Lieut., D.C.M., M.C. and Bar.
4562 Coward, W. G., Pte.
3279 Cox, A. H., Pte.
3363 Cox, C. R., Pte.
2796 Cox, F., L/Cpl.
3587 Cox, H., Sgt.
2880 Cox, R. Pte.
3366 Cox, T. J., Pte. M.M.
     Coyle, J., Lieut. M.M. and Bar, C. de G., Belgium.
3129 Cracknell, E. T., Pte.
2303 Crago, A., Pte.
1612 Craig, A. J., Sgt.
5354 Craig, G. D. R., Cpl.
3735 Craig, M. M., Pte.
1696 Craig, S., Pte.
 145 Craig, W., Pte.
2568 Creek, F. O., Pte.
4492 Crichton, H., Pte.
2399 Crain, J., Pte.
2395 Crain, R. T. S., Pte.
2879 Crane, P., Pte.
3279 Cravigan, R., Pte.
5358 Crawford, T. J., Dvr.
2632 Crawford, W. G., Pte.
4754 Crease, C., Pte.
3903 Creber, J. J., L/Cpl.
7868 Cridland, F. G., Pte.
7869 Cridland, H. C., Pte.
 363 Crighton, G. H., Pte.
54401 Crocker, H. E., Pte.
1682 Crocos, H. R., Pte.
3738 Crofton, H. E., Pte.
2148 Crome, C., Pte.
1935 Crooks, R., Pte.
     Crooks, T. R., 2/Lieut., M.C.
3275 Crookshanks, B. W., Dvr.
1726 Cropper, R., Pte.
2773 Cropper, S. C., Pte.
3261 Crosby, E., Pte.
1716 Cross, C. J., Pte.
4477 Crossan, W., L/Cpl.
4754 Crossman, E. A., Pte.
1619 Croucher, E. A., Pte.
2890 Croucher, N. R., Pte.

7041 Crowe, E., Pte.
(Alias Crowe, E. M.)
7050 Crowe, J. C., Pte.
7051 Crowe, J. H., Pte.
1927 Crowe, W. D., Pte.
4497 Crowl, R., Cpl.
4511 Croydon, A., Pte.
(Stated to be Elder, A. L.)
2398 Crozier, R. S., Pte.
3616 Cruickshank, D., Pte.
2356 Cruickshank, G., Pte.
5352 Cuddeford, E. L., Pte., M.M.
3028 Cuddy, J., Pte.
2357 Cullen, E. A., Sgt.
1652 Cullen, G., Sap.
2603 Cullen, J., Pte.
3120 Cullen, J. J., Pte.
1707 Culley, R., Pte.
2608 Cumming, H. S., Pte.
5356 Cummings, J., Pte.
2574 Cummins, C., Dvr.
3040 Cummins, T. G., Pte.
1690 Cundill, J. J., Pte.
306 Cunneen, J. A., Corp.
2432 Cunneen, W. J., Pte.
3365 Cunningham, G. H., Pte.
3620 Cunningham, J., Pte.
1665 Cupitt, E. J. G., Pte.
3498 Curel, A. C., Dvr.
7720 Curley, J. L., Pte.
2877 Curnock, T. L. L., Pte.
4166 Curran, C. E., Hon. Sgt., M.M.
4498 Curran, F., Pte.
1695 Currie, F., Pte.
1706 Curson, E. E., Sgt. M.M.
1326 Curtis, A. P., Sgt.
3529 Curtis, C. C., T/Cpl.
1730 Daddow, H. B., Pte.
2893 Dagwell, J. H., 2/AM.
2359 Dale, W., Pte.
3137 Dalliston, F. H., Pte.
5071 Daly, D. R., Pte.
1890 Daly, T., Dvr.
3748 Daniels, D. G., Pte.
846 Daniels, J. H., Pte.
3301 Dann, E. G., Pte.
3302 Dann, H. J., Pte.
4668 Dann, W. J., Sgt.
4356 Danswan, C. K., Sap.
3628 Dargan, J. H., Pte.
1733 Dargavalle, V., Gnr.
1666 Darnell, W. C., Pte.
1871 Darrell, E. N., Pte.
2896 Dartnell, R. J., Pte.
1937 Davenport, E., Pte.
3074 Davenport, H., Cpl.
4574 Davey, R. S., Pte.

7058 Davey, R. S., Pte.
3133 Davidson, C., T/Cpl. M.M.
4576 Davidson, J., Gnr.
1903 Davidson, R., Cpl., M.M.
3136 Davidson, T., Pte.
3375 Davidson, T., Pte.
2262 Davies, C. C., L/Cpl.
3749 Davies, D. T., Pte.
Davies, E., Capt. M.C.
3627 Davies, G. H., Pte.
2146 Davies, H., Sgt.
2408 Davies, J., Pte.
4798 Davies, J. L. H., T/Cpl.
3519 Davies, R., Pte.
2049 Davis, A., Pte.
3751 Davis, A. A., Gnr.
4900 Davis, C. H. R., Pte.
(Stated to be March, C. H. R.)
2820 Davis, E., Pte.
2168 Davis, G., Pte.
3373 Davis, G., Pte.
5364 Davis, G., Pte.
3030 Davis, H., Cpl.
4759 Davis, H. B., Pte.
3371 Davis, J. B., Pte.
4668 Davis, L., Pte.
2894 Davis, R. V., Pte.
5107 Davison, S. P. C., Pte.
7054 Dawes, A. J. T., Pte.
4499 Dawes, H. R., T/Cpl.
2167 Dawes, W. L., Pte.
4766 Daws, H., Pte.
2979 Dawson, B. J., Pte.
3558 Dawson, H., Spr.
2720 Dawson, H. C., Pte.
2739 Dawson, J. J., Pte.
3136 Dawson, P. R., Pte.
3983 Dawson, W. P., Pte. M.M.
2524 Day, J. H., Pte.
2406 Dayball, A. G., Pte.
2143 Dayball, P. F., Pte.
7055 Deale, L., Pte.
4475 Dean, C. A., Pte.
3374 Dean, C. R., Pte.
3631 Dearsley, E., Pte.
4761 De Belin, G. A., L/Cpl., M.M.
2160 De Bono, A., Pte.
3132 De Boynton, A., Pte.
7728 De Britt, M., Pte.
3753 Degotardi, F. D., Pte.
(Medaille Barba-tie si Credinta), (3rd Class) (Rou-mania)
7729 Delaney, A. J., Pte.
1716 Delaney, A. N., Pte.
3776 Deller, H. R., Pte.
2164 Dempster, J., Pte.
2409 Denham, H. C., Cpl.

3131 Denham, H. V., Pte.
54405 Denholm, A., Pte.
3998 Denny, H. T., T/Cpl.
4571 Denny, W. H., Cpl.
2363 Denson, W. M., L/Cpl.
7866 Dent, A. M., Pte.
1932 Denton, C., Pte.
4765 Denzel, A., T/Dvr. M.M.
3740 Dever, W. J., Pte.
998 Devine, M., Pte.
54408 De Wall, C. G., Pte.
20894 Dewhurst C. H., ER/Cpl.
2410 Diamond, T., Pte.
Dibbs, O. B., Capt.
1904 Dickson, J. H., Dvr.
2365 Dickson, R. A., Pte.
Dietze, J. H., 2nd Lt. (Stated to be Sandoe, J. H.)
3355 Dillon, H. T. C., Pte.
1911 Dinnerville, C. A., Pte.
2638 Ditton, G., Pte.
1729 Dixon, A. W., Pte.
3048 Dobbs, W. H., Pte.
3756 Dobson, A. L., Pte.
15077 Dodd, J. W., Pte.
1335 Doe, W. F., Sgt.
4681 Doggrell, H., Pte.
2404 Doherty, H., Pte.
3739 Doherty, J. J., Pte.
371 Doig, W. S., Sgt. M.M. (MI.D.)
2165 Dollisson, L. F., Pte.
Dolton, S. V., Lt.
2407 Don, W. E., Pte.
3130 Donald, W. I., L/Cpl.
54410 Donaldson, J. W., Gnr.
3755 Donaldson, W. J., Pte.
3629 Donegan, T., Pte.
4151 Donnelly, T., L/Cpl.
3738 Donnelly, W. A., Pte.
3539 Donovan, J. E., Pte.
21 Doolan, J. J. M. H., ER/2/Cpl.
3742 Dooley, H., Pte.
4573 Doran, J., Pte.
3038 Doran, J. C., L/Cpl.
1907 Dornan, J. L., Pte.
3741 Dorothy, W. F., Pte.
3584 Doughty, W. B., Pte.
2765 Douglas, A. B., Cpl.
2821 Douglas, N., Pte.
7183 Douglas, W. A., Pte.
15073 Dove, G. R., Pte.
3306 Dowd, P., Pte.
1906 Dowd, V. J., L/Cpl.
Dowding, A., Lt.
4575 Dowell, J. W., Pte.
1905 Dowling, C. E., L/Cpl.
2166 Dowling, J., Spr.
2895 Dowling, R. J., Pte.

4829 Fitzgerald, L. T., Pte.
3765 Fitzgerald, R. J., Dvr.
3042 Fitzgerald, T., Sergt. M.M. (M.I.D.)
     Fitzhardinge, A. C. B. Lieut., M.C.
3050 Fitzpatrick, J. A. P. Cpl.
2294 Flanagan, A., Pte.
7162 Flanagan, A. C., Pte.
2295 Flanagan, J. M., Pte.
730 Flanagan, P. J., Dvr.
2415 Flanigan, J., Pte.
2179 Flarey, V., Pte.
3639 Fleeting, H. W., Pte.
54422 Fleming, J. H., Mt/Dvr.
54424 Fletcher, D. A., Pte.
1918 Fletcher, F., L/Cpl.
4582 Fletcher, F. A., Pte.
3640 Fletcher, S., Sgt.
2175 Fletcher, W. T., Pte.
7731 Flick, B., Pte., M.M.
4294 Flynn, C. J., Pte.
724 Flynn, J., Pte.
2132 Foley, J., Pte.
3636 Forbes, C. B., Pte.
1917 Forbes, R., Corp.
2413 Ford, A. J., Pte.
     Ford, H. C., Maj., D.S.O. (5 M.I.D.)
2177 Ford, N. G., Pte.
4184 Ford, R. J. R., Pte.
3043 Ford, S., Dvr.
2903 Forrest, I. C., Pte.
2084 Forsyth, G. J., L/Cpl.
58724 Forsyth, H. J. H., Pte.
4186 Foster, O., Pte.
1383 Foster, W. E., Pte.
3314 Fowler, C. R., Sergt.
     Fowler, L., Lieut.
1135 Fowler, W., L/Cpl.
1753/1734 Fowler, Z. C., Corp.
3315 Fox, P., Pte.
7736 Frame, S., Pte.
3637 Frances, W. L., Pte.
3534 Francis, C. N., Sergt.
3638 Franklin, H. J., Pte.
54423 Frankum, W., Pte.
2376 Fraser, E., Corp.
5497 Fraser, P. P., Pte.
3142 Fraser, W., Pte.
7734 Frazer, D., Pte.
54417 Fred-Blad, H. W., Pte.
4776 Free, M. B., C.Q.M.S.
3141 Freeland, D. A. N., Pte.
3562 Freeman, H. A., Pte.
608 Freeman, R. W., Corp.
7062 French, W. A., Pte.
3367 Frost, A., Pte.
7063 Frost, A. W., Pte.

     Frost, G. A. J., Lieut., M.M.
3146 Frost, L. S., E.R./2/Cpl (M.I.D.)
7735 Frusher, G. A., Pte.
2174 Fuller, P. R., Pte.
2377 Funnell, J. P., Corp.
3377 Furness, C. E., Pte.
3516 Gabriel, A. F., Pte.
7746 Gabriel, W. B., Pte.
     Gadsby, H. P., Lieut.
3148 Gaffney, P. J., Pte.
2334 Gain, A., Pte.
2335 Gain, R. S., Pte.
2915 Galbraith, J. R., Pte.
4032 Gallagher, J., Pte.
7742 Gallagher, J., Pte.
7173 Gallagher, W. F., Pte.
1343 Gallegos, H. G., Pte.
1667 Galliven, D., Corpl. (M.I.D.)
3335 Gallop, G. H., Pte., M.M.
3779 Galloway, I. C., Pte.
428 Galloway, S. T., Pte.
3151 Gardner, C. H., Dvr.
1734 Gardner, J., Pte.
7065 Gardner, R. W., Pte.
     Garling, L., Lieut., (M.I.D.)
2185 Gardner, A., Pte.
2011 Garner, G. A., Pte.
     Garnett, W. S., Maj.
1691 Garratt, J. H., Pte.
506 Garred, A. D., Sergt.
3569 Gass, H. G., Pte.
7739 Gavin, W., Pte.
4813 Gaylard, T. R., Pte.
4589 Geary, J., Gunner.
2833 Geary, P. B., L/Cpl. M.M.
4189 Geddes, A. R., Pte.
7745 Geelan, J. C., Pte.
2059 Geer, G. S., Gunner.
3150 Gemmell, W. B., Pte.
2520 George, R. W., Corp.
4446 George, S. A., Pte.
3754 Geraghty, C. E., Pte.
2910 Gerard, D. A., Pte.
5376 Ghilardi, G., Pte.
2510 Gibb, J., Pte.
3783 Gibbins, R., Bombdr.
2758 Gibbons, T. W., Pte.
1919 Gibbs, F. J., Pte.
2421 Gibson, E Pte.
3525 Gibson, W., Pte., M.M.
2738 Gibson, W. A., Pte.
2368 Gibsone, G., L/Cpl.
1638 Giddins, W. H., Pte.
4439 Gilberd, W., T/Sgt.
4213 Gilbert, A., Pte.
     Gilder, G., Chaplain/Capt.
4190 Giles, W. G., Sergt.
3641 Giles, C. P., Pte.

3325 Gillard, R. A., Pte.
3283 Gillard, W., Pte.
4807 Gillespie, T., Pte.
19581 Gillett, H., Pte.
     Gillies, R. T., Lieut.
732 Gilmore, M., Pte.
2180 Gilroy, H. P., Pte.
2767 Ginn, A. A., Pte.
3260 Glassbrook, T., Pte.
4196 Glazebrook, H., Pte.
2420 Gleadhill, F. W., Pte.
1730 Gleaves, J., Pte.
2000 Gluyas, P., Corp.
4030 Goard, R. D., Pte.
     Gocher, W. W., 2/Lieut., M.M. and Bar.
1448 Goidman, J. W., Sergt.
2652 Godwin, C., Pte.
3775 Goff, J. F., Dvr.
2913 Golden, J. E. J., Sergt., D.C.M.
2291 Goldenberg, L. S., Corp.
2001 Goldsworthy, W. J., Pte.
2836 Goode, E., Pte.
2418 Goodman, C. H., Pte.
3379 Goodwin, F. J., Pte.
255 Goodwin, P. H. R., Pte.
2829 Goodwin, K. B., R.Q.M.S.
2907 Goodwin, V. L., Pte.
1684 Gooley, J., Pte.
4781 Gooley, P., Pte.
2912 Gordon, E. V., Pte.
3017 Gordon, J. E., Pte.
4507 Gordon, J. P., Pte.
2149 Gordon, L. A., Pte.
3380 Gore, G. T., L/Cpl.
2422 Gorman, M., Pte.
3785 Gorman, T. J., Sergt.
2417 Gornall, S., Pte.
2182 Gosper, V. J., Sergt. D.C.M.
3772 Gottery, R. P., L/Cpl.
3321 Gough, B. R., Gun.
1731 Gould, A. L., Pte.
3322 Gould, E., Gunner.
2914 Goulden, J., Pte.
1746 Gow, D., Pte.
4504 Gow, R. D., Pte.
     Gowing, R. L., Lieut.
3780 Gowley, G. A., Dvr.
7066 Goyen, E. R., Pte.
2588 Graham, G. C., Corp.
2435 Graham, J., Pte.
1739 Graham, S. F., Pte.
2645 Grainger, D. H., Pte.
3047 Grant, C. S. C., Fitter.
853 Grant, J., Dvr.
1735 Grant, J. A., L/Cpl.

4620 Gratton, G. H., Corp. M.M.
1815 Grave, J. C., Pte.
4170 Graves, J., L/Cpl.
2835 Gray, A. H., Corp.
5379 Gray, C. H., Pte.
2908 Gray, F. V., Pte.
54428 Gray, G., Pte.
1920 Gray, J. L., Pte.
3282 Gray, H. S. R., Pte.
4169 Gray, W., Pte
2181 Grear, W., L/Cpl. M.M.
5676 Green, A. E., Pte.
3326 Green, P., Pte.
Green, R. C., Lieut.
2186 Green, R. W. G., Pte.
20911 Green, W., Pte.
3479 Greenwood, A. L. Sergt., D.C.M., M.M.
2641 Gregory, J. F., Pte.
2644 Grey, W. V., Pte.
54426 Grieve, W. C., T/Cpl.
Griffin, H. N., Lieut.
3929 Griffiths, E., Pte.
4785 Griffiths, G. M., Pte.
1620 Griffiths, H., Pte.
1903 Griffiths, H. F., Pte.
2642 Griffiths, N. A., Pte.
2640 Griffiths, W. C., Pte.
1904 Griffiths, W. S., Pte.
165 Griggs, F., Gunner.
2651 Grigg, W. E., Pte.
2909 Grills, W. E., Pte.
3149 Grogan, R. G., Pte.
3532 Grogin, W., Pte.
1739 Gronow, D. H., Dvr.
1872 Guegan, L., Pte.
4587 Gunn, W., Gunner.
3765 Gunning, S. C., Pte.
2161 Gunns, H. A., Pte.
7743 Gurney, J., Pte.
3317 Guthrie, J. J., Pte.
3990 Guy, J., Pte.
2183 Glynn, A. A. C., Pte.
2630 Hadaway, T. W., Pte.
7749 Haddock, R., Pte.
2528 Haebich, F., Pte., D.C.M., M.M.
3787 Haggerwood, F. I., Corp. M.M.
7070 Hailwood, E. P., Pte.
2434 Haines, A. A., Pte.
2608 Haines, H. E., Corp.
2433 Haines, H. J. L., Pte.
1705 Hair, A. E., T/Dvr.
2385 Halgren, A. A., Corp.
1701 Hall, A., Pte.
4039 Hall, G. P. C., Pte.
2769 Hall, H. W., Pte.
1907 Hall, J., Sergt.
4197 Hall, J., Pte., M.M.
3331 Hall, O., Pte.

3382 Hall, T. G., L/Cpl.
2916 Hall, V. B., Pte.
4795 Hall, W., Pte.
1937 Hall, W. H., Pte.
62 Halle, C. E., E.R./ Sgt., M.S.M.
395 Halley, W., Pte.
2024 Halliday, W. E., Corp.
7748 Hallinan, M., Pte. (Stated to be Hallinan, Martin.)
2376 Hally, J., Pte.
2428 Halpin, T. A., Pte.
1693 Hamer, H., Pte.
2948 Hamer, J. E., Pte.
1090 Hamilton, C S., Pte.
5393 Hamilton, G. B., Pte.
2842 Hamilton, J., Pte.
1926 Hamilton, T. E., Pte.
2352 Hamilton, W. H., Sapper.
4835 Hamling, J. J., Pte.
2924 Hammond, H. A., Pte.
2432 Hamon, G., Pte.
3332 Hampstead, A. W., Pte.
1752 Hampton, W. H., Pte.
7760 Hanagan, W., E.R./ 2/Cpl.
1927 Hancock, P. A., Sergt., D.C.M.
4444 Hand, D., Sergt.
Hand, J. A., Capt.
3799 Handel, E. A., Pte.
3265 Handfield, P., Pte.
54441 Hanks, R. T., Pte.
2655 Hann, A. A., Pte.
2196 Hannam, W. H., Pte.
Hannay, D. V., Maj.
4199 Hannelly, P. A., Pte.
1952 Hannon, W. T., Pte.
2651 Hansen, C. T., Pte.
3140 Hansen, J., Pte.
4445 Hansen, N. J., Pte.
4201 Hansen, P. N., C.Q.M.S.
1923 Hansen, V. E., Pte.
2919 Hansford, J. C. M., Pte.
3518 Hanson, H. M., Pte.
3341 Harder, R. C., Pte.
1759 Hardie, D., Pte.
2653 Hardie, H., Pte.
4201 Hardie, R. G., Pte.
1630 Harding, B. A., E.R./2/Cpl.
2846 Harding, F. G., Dvr.
Hardley, W., T/Capt.
2956 Harlow, C., Pte.
15482 Harper, W., Pte.
1726 Harrick, J., Pte.
7751 Harries, H. J. G., Pte.

7076 Harrington, G. P., Pte.
3791 Harris, C., Pte.
3162 Harris, E. M., Pte.
3642 Harris, F., Pte.
3801 Harris, F. G., Corp.
1924 Harris, F. L. D., Pte.
1550 Harris, G., Pte.
1669 Harris, H., Pte.
2431 Harris, J. H., Pte.
3158 Harris, M., Pte.
394 Harris, R. S., Pte.
2290 Harris, W. A. R., Pte., D.C.M.
3057 Harrison, A. R., Pte.
3789 Harrison, B. H., Pte.
2774 Harrison, H. C., Pte.
350 Harrison, H. D., Pte.
2775 Harrison, O. L., Pte.
5042 Harrison, R., Pte.
2386 Harrison, W. J., Gun.
7075 Hartland, E., Pte.
1922 Hartley, A. N., Pte.
1925 Harvey, A. H. Pte.
3345 Harvey, C. W., Pte.
1732 Harvey, F. J., Pte.
4511 Harvie, W. C., Pte.
3055 Harwood, J. M., L/Cpl.
19529 Haseler, T. M., Pte.
4793 Haskett, T. W., Pte.
2424 Hatch, T. H., Pte.
7177 Hathaway, G., Pte.
3298 Hatherley, W. H., Pte.
5386 Hawes, J. E., Pte.
54430 Hawke, L. S., Pte.
5092 Hawkes, O. S., Pte.
2647 Hawkes, S., Pte.
4794 Hawkins, A. C., Pte.
7763 Hawkins, G. J., Pte.
5382 Hay, S. J., Pte.
2766 Hayes, G. E., Pte.
1751 Hayes, R., Pte.
14744 Hayhow, W. H., Pte.
3163 Haynes, F. A., Pte.
3806 Hayward, W. J., Pte.
2423 Hazelton, L. W., Pte.
3036 Hazelton, S., Pte., M.M.
1928 Hazelwood, A., Pte.
Hazelwood, F. H., Lieut., M.M.
3334 Hazlewood, L. W., Pte.
4505 Heading, J. A., R.S.M., D.C.M., M.M.
3071 Healey, M. W. R., Pte.
3802 Healey, A., Pte.
2513 Heap, J. E. T., L/Cpl.
2190 Heard, R. H., Pte.

Mashford, R. L., Lieut., Medaille Militaire, French. (M.I.D.)

15495 Mashman, H. W. E.R./2/Cpl.
7797 Masling, E., Pte.
2935 Masman, A. R., Pte.
2679 Masman, J. C., Pte.
3671 Mason, A. H., Pte.
3837 Mason, A. L., Pte.
1649 Mason, G. E., L/Cpl.
1956 Mason, H. H., Pte.
4656 Mason, J. J., Pte.
3378 Massey, G., Pte.
3084 Masters, J. J., Pte.
3200 Masters, R. E., Pte.
3677 Masterton, V. W., Pte.
2284 Mather, E., Pte.
2644 Mathers, J. W., Dvr.
5074 Matheson, R. B., Pte.
3392 Mathisen, O., Pte.
3409 Mathews, F., Pte., M.M.
2291 Matthews, F. T., Pte.
2883 Matthews, G. A., Pte.
1965 Matthews, W. J., Pte.
3391 Matthews, W. J., Pte.
2652 Mattson, F., Pte.
1776 Maude, G. S. W., L/Cpl.
3418 Maude, T., L/Cpl.
1157 Maule, C., L/Cpl.
1701 Maurer, E. O., Dvr.
2208 May, E., L/Cpl.
3411 May, S. St. T., Pte.
5075 Mayers, G. D., Pte.
1371 Mayne, W. H., Sergt.
7802 Meacle, R. G., Pte.
3206 Meadows, L. M., Pte.
Mear, H., Lieut.
1667 Meeks, J. R., Pte.
1740 Meers, C. R., Pte.
1715 Meers, V. E., L/Cpl.
Meggitt, W. T., Lieut.
4255 Meldrum, A. O., Dvr.
2946 Melchan, P., Pte.
2412 Mellon, E. G., Dvr.
1993 Melrose, W., Pte.
1382 Melton, C. W., Pte.
2211 Melville, T. H., L/Cpl.
5135 Mephan, S. H. H., Pte.
7093 Merchant, W., Pte.
4642 Meredith, A. C., Pte.
2677 Meredith, E. T., Pte.
2178 Meredith, R. L., Pte. (Stated to be Falconer, R.)
1792 Merrison, C., Pte.
2455 Merz, A. J., Pte.
1795 Mexted, R. R., Pte.

3839 Meyers, R. C. L., Pte.
2683 Meyers, W. H., Pte.
3207 Michie, W. A., Pte.
3483 Middlemiss, R. M., Pte.
3205 Milburn, G., Pte. (Stated to be Johncke, G. T.)
3674 Miles, E. G., Pte.
1986 Miles, R. W., Pte.
538 Milgate, J., Gunner.
1959 Millar, A. McD., Pte.
3377 Millar, H. J., Pte.
2653 Millar, W. B. R., Corpl.
1784 Millard, T. W., Gun.
4238 Miller, A., Pte.
3840 Miller, E. F., Dvr.
4844 Miller, G., Corpl.
2209 Miller, W. E., Pte.
1958 Miller, W. F., Pte.
3100 Miller, W. N., Pte.
3420 Millet, R. B., Sapper
3669 Milligan, J., Pte.
1747 Milligan, P., Pte.
Mills, A. M., Lieut.
2210 Mills, G. E., Pte.
3514 Mills, R., Pte.
3203 Milne, R., Pte.
1450 Milner, R. P., Dvr.
3842 Milsop, A. J., Dvr.
3673 Milton, G., Pte. (Stated to be Caddy, A. M. G.)
3199 Miners, S. H. O., Pte.
1966 Mini, J., Pte.
Minty, R. J., Lieut., M.C., M.M. (M.I.D.)
3414 Mitchell, A. S., Pte.
2683 Mitchell, C. B., Pte.
15284 Mitchell, E. C., Pte.
2678 Mitchell, G. E., Pte.
Mitchell, H. F., 2/Lieut.
2646 Mitchell, J., Gunner.
1736 Mitchell, L. E., E.R./2/Cpl.
3289 Mitchell, P. H., Pte.
5153 Mitchell, R. F. Z., E.R./Sgt.
2748 Mitchell, W. T., Pte.
3848 Mole, A., Pte.
2160 Moller, P., Pte.
5417 Monaghan, W. C., T/Dvr.
3957 Monahan, M., Pte.
4082 Moncrieff, E. W., Pte.
1669 Monk, E., Pte.
7799 Montefiore, S. R., Pte.
539 Montgomery, J. D., Sergt.
3480 Moody, J., Pte.
2951 Moore, A. E., Pte.

Moore, B. R., Lieut., M.C.
2675 Moore, C. A., Pte.
3164 Moore, C. H., Pte.
3288 Moore, H. T. J., Pte.
2949 Moore, J., F., Pte. (Alias Moir, J. F.)
4966 Moore, S. G., Dvr.
2731 Moore, W., Dvr.
1686/5054 Moore, W. D., Pte.
4610 Moore, W. S. T., Bombdr.
4242 Moorhouse, S. J., Pte.
760 Moran, J., Pte.
3675 Moran, J., J., Pte.
3394 Morell, G. L. C., Pte.
Morell, J. F., Lieut.
Morgan, A. E., Capt.
1029 Morgan, C., Sergt.
2952 Morgan, C. F., Pte.
5409 Morgan, F., Pte.
5080 Morgan, L., Pte.
2000 Morgan, R., Pte.
4517 Morgan, R., Corpl. M.M.
2922 Morley, C. C., Pte.
1782 Morley, G. H., Pte.
3875 Moroney, B. J. P., L/Cpl.
Moroney, J. T., Lt.
3372 Moroney, W. J., Pte.
2201 Morrey, W. E., Pte.
2460 Morris, A. W., Pte.
26 Morris, E. W., Pte.
5411 Morris, E. R., Pte.
2944 Morris, W., Pte.
4849 Morris, J., Pte.
1789 Morris, J. J., Pte.
3546 Morris, K., Pte.
2212 Morrish, J., Pte.
3845 Morrison, C., Pte.
3421 Morrison, F. J., Pte.
1668 Morrison, G. H., Corpl.
2773 Morrison, J., Pte.
2960 Morrison, J. P., Pte.
3672 Morrissey, C., Pte.
3379 Morrissey, J., Pte.
1775 Morrow, G. E., Pte.
4561 Mortimer, A., Pte., M.M.
4243 Morton, S. J., Pte.
Morton, V., Lieut., M.C.
2153 Moseley, E. C., Sgt.
7021 Mosley, H. A., Pte.
196 Moss, C. R., L/Cpl.
2221 Moss, H., L/Cpl.
1961 Mossop, C. D., Pte.
1962 Mossop, S. S., Pte.
3187 Mott, H. S., E.R./2/Cpl.
1696 Moule, F. S., Pte.

1960 Mourney, A. J., E.R./2/Cpl.
2873 Mowatt, T., Corpl.
441 Moylan, W. P., Pte.
4244 Mudie, G. T., Pte.
Muir, A. R., Lieut., M.C.
3883 Muir, J., Pte.
755 Mulholland, J. S., L/Cpl.
3399 Mulholland, W. T., Dvr.
3386 Mulley, J., Pte.
2037 Mulligan, T. P., Pte.
2214 Munday, E. J., L/Cpl.
2290 Munday, S. H., Pte.
3209 Munger, A., Pte.
2459 Mungomery, G., Pte.
4246 Munn, A. H., Corpl.
5413 Munn, H. W., Pte.
2956 Munro, C. A., Pte.
4602 Munro, D., Pte.
744 Munro, G., Pte.
7887 Munro, J. H., Pte.
2955 Munro, S. A., Pte.
1362 Munro, W., Pte.
2874 Murkin, P. A., Pte.
5128 Murphy, C. R., Pte.
2948 Murphy, F. L., Pte.
2457 Murphy, H. E., Pte.
7798 Murphy, J., Pte.
3189 Murphy, N. A., Pte.
3751 Murray, F. T., Pte.
1963 Murray, H., Pte.
5415 Murray, H., Pte.
Murray, P. V., Lieut.
Murray, R. A. M., Lieut., M.C.
3204 Murray, R. V. M., L/Cpl.
615 Murray, S. P., Corpl.
43419 Murray, W., Pte.
54466 Murrell, D., Pte.
2188 Murry, J. J., Pte.
1994 Murtagh, A. J., Pte.
2456 Muscat, W., Pte.
3670 Musgrave, B., Pte.
2673 Musgrave, W., Pte.
3856 Musgrove, T. H., L/Cpl.
2875 Myles, J. K., Corpl.
3967 MacAuley, J., L/Cpl.
4248 MacAuley, R. O., Pte.
MacDiarmid, A. M., Lieut.
MacDonald, A. K., 2/Lieut.
2491 MacDonald, A. N., Pte.
1133 MacDonald, J., Pte.
3398 MacDonald, R. W., Pte.
2790 MacDougall, C. F., Corpl.

2690 MacFarlane, H., Pte.
3853 MacGregor, R. K., Corpl., M.M.
2860 MacIver, A., T/Sgt. M.M.
3202 Mack, J., Pte.
3852 Mackay, J., Pte.
981 Mackenzie, C. J., Corpl.
3686 Mackenzie, N. A., Pte.
3760 Mackenzie, J. F., Pte.
3854 Mackenzie, W. J., 2nd A.M.
3020 Mackey, C., Pte.
4375 Mackie, E. T., Corpl.
4514 Mackie, J., Pte.
1708 Mackie, W. J., Pte.
2692 MacLean, J. D., Pte.
2421 MacLeod, M., Pte.
2452 MacNab, A. G., Mt./Dvr.
3173 MacPherson, N., Pte.
4669 MacRae, G. E., Pte.
2953 McAlister, A., Pte.
2688 McAuliffe, T. W., Pte.
3195 McBean, W., Pte.
2777 McBride, M., Pte., M.M.
2641 McCabe, J., Pte.
4827 McCarter, J., Pte.
2945 McCarthy, L. H., Pte.
3421 McBride, M., Pte.
4197 McCarron, W. J., Pte.
2787 McCloy, M., Pte.
417 McColl, W. N., Sgt.
3679 McCollin, W. H., Pte.
5144 McConville, A. J., Pte.
3416 McConville, J. H., Pte.
7831 McCormack, C. R. T.
4249 McCormick, J., Pte. (Stated to be Cormick, J. B.)
2882 McCoughtry, R. W., L/Cpl.
4662 McCoullough, N. E., Pte.
2648 McCowen, R. R., Pte.
7793 McCoy, R., Pte.
3683 McCrory, W. H., Pte.
3402 McCrow, D. E., Pte.
1735 McCue, C., Pte.
5423 McCusker, H., L/Cpl. M.M.
2475 McDonald, A., L/Cpl.
7790 McDonald, A., Pte.

6852 McDonald, A. F., Pte.
3362 McDonald, D., Corpl.
McDonald, E. F., Lieut.
2958 McDonald, F. E., Corpl., M.M.
2957 McDonald, G. C., Pte.
2959 McDonald, J., Pte.
3090 McDonald, J. N., Pte.
2375 McDonald, P. A., L/Cpl.
McDonald, S., Lieut.
3409 McDonald, V. R., Pte. (should read MacDonald.)
3684 McDonald, W., Pte.
4001 McDonnell, J. W. L., Pte.
4087 McDonnell, W. H., Pte.
1996 McDonough, P., Gun.
1556 McDonough, W. M., Pte.
3987 McDougall, C. L., Pte.
3680 McDowell, H. A., Pte.
2462 McEachern, G. E., Pte.
1819 McErlain, J., L/Cpl.
3192 McEvoy, A. E., Pte.
2002 McFadden, F. A., Pte., M.M.
3198 McFadden, R. J., Pte.
3860 McFarland, E., Pte.
3864 McFarlane, F. W., Dvr.
15078 McGarry, F. J., Pte.
7789 McGaw, R. F., Pte.
7092 McGee, F. T., Pte.
2175 McGee, J. P., Pte.
2770 McGillycuddy, T., Pte.
2735 McGillivray, G., Pte.
2955 McGlinchey, M., L/Cpl.
2454 McGlynn, W. S., Pte.
4943 McGowan, B. C., Pte.
4562 McGrath, B. D., Cpl., M.M.
1967 McGrath, H. V., Pte.
1654 McGrath, L. J., L/Cpl.
4037 McGrath, P. J., Pte.
3197 McGrath, W., Pte.
2657 McGregor, C. H., L/Cpl.
2886 McGregor, O. J., Pte.
1696 McGregor, S., Corpl. M.M.
2064 McGregor, W. G., Pte.

3194 McGuire, H., Pte.
4857 McGuire, J. R., Pte.
2947 McHugh, C., Pte.
2453 McIlwraith, P. E., Pte.
2962 McInnes, G. F., Pte.
1381 McInnes, J., Pte.
3865 McInnes, J., Pte.
3095 McInnes, R. G., Pte.
4251 McInnes, W. A., Pte.
1968 McIntosh, W., Pte.
7782 McIntyre, C. F., Pte.
     McIntyre, T. A., Lieut. ,
6853 McIvor, H. H., Pte.
3092 McKane, J., C.S.M.
3560 McKay, C., Pte.
1799 McKay, D., Pte.
3154 McKay, H. N., Sgt.
3361 McKay, T. E., Pte.
     McKay, W. A., Lieut.
4561 McKean, J. J., Pte.
2691 McKell, J. T., Pte.
2950 McKenna, C. E., Pte.
4605 McKenna, V. H., Pte.
411 McKenna, W., Pte.
2687 McKenzie, A., Pte.
2942 McKenzie, A. H., Pte.
2276 McKenzie, A. W., Pte.
1381 McKenzie, H., Pte.
2963 McKenzie, H. A., Pte.
     McKenzie, J. G., Lieut.
     McKenzie, J. R., Lieut., M.M.
4862 McKeown, J., Pte.
     McKinley, T. J., Lieut., M.S.M.
3474 McLachlan G. P., Pte.
4252 McLachlan. G. R., L/Cpl.
5420 McLean, A., Pte.
2686 McLean, C. H., Pte.
4522 McLean, C. W., Pte.
3694 McLean, E. N., Pte.
1801 McLean, H. A. S., Dvr.
     McLean, J. L., Lieut.
3645 McLean, R. W., Pte.
1162 McLean, W., Pte.
1782 McLeod, D., Pte.
3862 McLeod, E. K., Corpl.
3193 McLeod, H. C., Pte.
4666 McLoskey, H. L., Sergt.
3505 McMahon, E., Pte.
3415 McMahon, E. R., Pte.
4501 McMahon, F., Pte.

     McMahon, R. G. F., Lieuten., M.C., (M.I.D.)
2378 McManus, M. J., Sergt., M.M.
5425 McManus, O., Pte.
2949 McMaster, W. J., Pte.
3009 McMicken, L. S., Pte.
2874 McMillan, A., Pte.
2940 McMillan, A., Sergt.
3417 McMillan, A. A., Pte.
4861 McMillan, C. R., Pte.
7103 McMillan, J. N., Pte.
1644 McNabb, J. T., Pte.
200 McNamara, B., Pte.
2176 McNamara, C., Pte.
3407 McNamara, E. E., E.R./Sgt.
1756 McNamara, F. A., Pte.
2739 McNamara, P. J., L/Cpl.
3646 McNamee, J., Pte.
1382 McNaught, R., Pte.
4860 McNeil, G. R., Pte.
4609 McNeil, W. J., Pte.
2957 McNeill, D. G., Corp.
3285 McNeill, J. W. A., Corpl.
2689 McNellee, S., Pte.
     McNiven, C. R., Lieut.
3196 McParland, W., Pte.
3191 McPhee, J. M. J., Pte.
2954 McPhee, N. C., Pte.
3096 McQuarrie, A. A., Pte.
2695 Nabi Bux, J. C., Pte.
2215 Nairne, T. H., Pte.
2759 Nankervis, W., Pte.
3689 Napier, S. J., Pte.
3211 Napper, C. E., Pte.
54484 Nasstrom, H. H., Pte.
2964 Neame, A. D., Pte.
1416 Neary, C. P., Pte.
     Neaves, H. H., Lieut. & Hon. Capt., M.C.
3425 Neill, J., Pte.
3212 Neilley, J. C., Pte.
4216 Neilson, H. D., Pte.
3866 Neilson, J., Pte.
2661 Neilson, N., Pte.
3688 Neilson, R. A., Pte.
3687 Nelson, S. G., Pte.
2965 Nesbit, H. P., Pte.
4613 Nesbitt, G. C., Pte.
4863 Nettleton, H. T., Pte.
5142 Newberry, T. H., L/Cpl.

1969 Newland, J. F., T/Dvr.
74 Newman, J., Corpl.
5154 Newnham, N. H., Corpl.
2890 Newson, A. H. P., Bombdr.
3691 Newsum, W., Pte.
4611 Newton, J. C., Pte.
1704 Nicholls, A. S., Pte.
1971 Nicholls, C., T/Sgt.
3690 Nicholls, L., Pte.
1367 Nicholls, W. J., L/Cpl.
7517 Nicholson, D. A., Pte.
2966 Nicholson, J. M., Pte.
4612 Nicholson, W. W., Pte.
858 Nickisson, A. G. G., Pte.
5427 Nickson, T., L/Cpl., M.M.
2889 Nicol, D. R., L/Cpl., Dvr.
3213 Nicoll. C. C. F., Pte. (Stated to be O'Brien, M.)
1970 Nicoll, O. G., Pte.
2463 Nicolls, G. A., Pte., M.M.
2917 Nielsen, H. K. A., Pte., M.M.
2968 Nightingale, F., Pte. (Stated to be Nightingale, R. A.)
1709 Nigro, J., Pte.
4520 Nix, W. H., Gunner. M.M.
5428 Nixon, S., J., Pte.
4551 Noakes, R. S., Pte.
2216 Nobbs, I. S., Pte.
2694 Nobes, A., Pte.
3495 Noble, A., Pte.
4392 Noble, J. J., Pte.
2457 Noble, R. E., Pte.
5429 Nolan, W. J., Pte.
514 Noonan, W. J., Sergt.
1676 Norbery, H. H., Pte.
764 Norman, R., Pte.
1808 Norris, C. J., Corpl.
2211 Norris, W. E., Dvr.
1973 North, G. H., A/Sgt.
3270 Notley, J. S., Pte.
1972 Nott, C. E., Pte.
19549 Nott, K. G., Sapper.
4217 Noud, R., Dvr.
4823 Nugent, B. L., Pte.
1705 Nugent, J., Pte.
3011 O'Brien, F. A., Pte.
3874 O'Brien, G. E., Gun.
4521 O'Brien, J., Corpl.
2285 O'Brien, J. F., Pte.
7864 O'Brien, J. T., Pte.
2776 O'Connell, D., Pte.

3692 O'Connell, D., Pte.
3693 O'Connor, A. L., Pte.
1645 O'Connor, G. W., L/Cpl.
1749 O'Connor, J., Pte.
1637 O'Connor, M., Pte.
1663 O'Connor, P., Pte.
2217 O'Connor, T., Pte.
7106 O'Connor, T. P., Pte.
1974 Odgers, J. R., Far/Cpl.
4586 O'Donnell, H. B., T/Mt/Dvr.
3566 O'Donnell, H. R., Pte.
2634 O'Donnell, J., Pte.
4559 O'Donnell, J., Pte.
548 O'Donnell, J. R., Sergt., D.C.M.
2535 O'Dwyer, T. F., Pte.
3421 Ogilvie, J. M., Pte.
1635 Ogle, F. J., L/Cpl.
15272 O'Hehir, J. R., Pte.
3874 Ohlsen, W. J., Pte.
4647 Oldfield, E. J., Pte.
1433 Oldfield, F. R., L/Sgt., M.M.
5231 Oldfield, J. A., Pte.
Olds, O. A., Lieut.
2217 Oliver, G. R., Pte.
1710 Oliver, T. J., Pte.
3006 Oliver, W. C., Pte., D.C.M.
7805 Olliffe, R. D., T/Mt/Dvr.
3420 Olliffe, W. R., Pte.
3216 O'Loughlin, M. P., Pte.
3873 Olsen, O. V., Sergt., D.C.M. (M.I.D.)
4614 O'Mara, O. C., Pte.
2010 O'Meara, H. J., Corpl.
1748 O'Meara, J., Pte.
3029 O'Meara, J. M., Pte.
4459 Omondo, W., S/Sgt.
O'Reilly, P. D., Lieut., M.M.
3437 O'Reilly, S. P., Dvr.
2716 O'Reilly, S. V., Sgt.
2970 Oriel, W. J., Pte.
3424 Osborn, W., Pte.
2663 Osborne, C., L/Cpl.
2696 Osborne, T. E., Pte.
4573 Overend, A. S., Pte.
3515 Overman, E. J., Pte.
7807 Owen, H., Pte. (Stated to be Owen, R.)
2740 Owen, J., Pte.
3217 Owen, L. H. O., Corpl.
1714 Owens, A. E. N., Pte.
206 Owens, R., Pte.

4060 Owens, W. R., Pte.
2464 Oxley, V., Pte.
3872 Ozard, J. P., L/Cpl.
3883 Page, P. C., Pte.
2266 Page, W. F., Pte., M.M.
3103 Paine, J. T., Sergt.
3189 Paine, S. C., Pte.
4268 Palmer, E., Pte.
3430 Palmer, J. R., Pte.
3016 Palmer, S. G., L/Cpl. M.M.
1659 Palmer, W. J., Pte.
3432 Palmgren, J. I., Pte.
2223 Park, J., Pte.
Parke, G. P. S., Lieut.
4463 Parke, R. A. L., Bombdr.
2975 Parker, A. G., Pte.
1687 Parker, A. J., Pte.
3695 Parker, J., Pte.
3694 Parker, J. E., Pte.
1823 Parker, J. H., Pte.
2470 Parker, J. H., Pte.
Parker, K. S., Maj., M.C.
1611 Parker, L. E., Pte.
15087 Parker, S. E., Pte.
3486 Parkes, C., Pte.
2220 Parkes, S., Corpl.
2972 Parks, H. C., Pte.
2973 Parks, J. H., Pte.
4871 Parlett, T. H., Corpl.
3433 Parnell, J., Pte.
2667 Parry, T., Pte.
Parsons, F. E., Lieut., M.C.
3698 Parsons, S., Pte.
1330 Partridge, C. D., E.R./Cpl.
4589 Passmore, G., Pte.
208 Paterson, A., Pte.
Paterson, F. A., Lieut.
Paterson, M., 2/Lieut.
3434 Patman, E. W., Pte.
2970 Patmore, J., Pte.
1711 Patrick, J., Pte.
3875 Patten, J., Pte.
3431 Patterson, W. A., Pte.
4572 Patterson, W. J., L/Cpl., M.M.
2279 Pattison, F., Dvr.
3272 Patton, N. J., Pte.
1442 Paul, D., L/Cpl C. de G., Belgian.
4268 Paul, L. W. C., Pte.
7109 Paull, C. S., Pte.
5436 Paver, H., Pte.
4265 Payne, A. E., L/Cpl.
2703 Payne, H., Pte.
2224 Payne, H. A., Pte.
3106 Payne, T. H., Gun.
1834 Peach, E. F., L/Cpl.

3592 Pearce, B. L., Pte.
5435 Pearce, J. H., Pte.
2219 Pearce, J. J., Pte.
4872 Pearce, L., Pte.
4266 Pearce, P. C., Pte.
1654 Pearson, A. V., Pte.
3697 Pearson, E. E., Pte.
1750 Pearson, L., Pte.
3435 Peck, E., L/Cpl.
2466 Peden, W. K., E.R./2/Cpl.
1976 Pedersen, L. C., Pte.
4314 Peebles, J. H., Pte.
2486 Peirce, A. G. R., Pte.
3715 Pelissier, F. L., Pte.
7110 Pender, L. G., Pte.
2219 Pendleton, F., Pte.
5433 Penny, A., Pte.
1697 Penny, R. M., Pte.
4628 Pentecost, R. W Corpl.
2425 Pentland, B. L., Pte.
2222 Perkins, H. G., Pte., M.M.
2198 Perriman, F. J., Pte.
3699 Perrott, C., Pte.
Perry, J. R. S., Lt.
3105 Perry, R. B., Pte.
Perry, S. L., Lt./Col., D.S.O., M.C. (M.I.D. 4.)
1545 Perry, V., Dvr.
2698 Perston, J. R., Pte.
4918 Petch, A., Pte.
2472 Peters, A. F., Pte.
9805 Peters, R. E., Pte.
3507 Peterson, C. A., Pte.
2976 Petrie, C. S., L/Cpl.
4876 Pettigrew, R. W., Pte.
4594 Petty, A. T. A. W., Pte.
2235 Peverill, J., Pte.
7185 Phelan, E., Pte.
3434 Phelan, J. J., Pte.
7111 Phelan, V., Pte.
2468 Phelps, E. W., Pte.
Philip, S. A., Lieut.
3478 Philips, G., Pte.
1977 Philipson, F. J., Pte.
1036 Phillips, F. J., Pte.
2704 Phillips, G. G. T. R.
4615 Phillips, J. A., Sgt.
2465 Phillips, J. H., Pte.
2536 Phipps, H., Pte.
3700 Pickering, A. H., Pte.
5432 Pickering, A. J., Pte.
2701 Pickering, F. A., Pte.
Pickup, R. S., Hon./Capt., M.C.
2471 Pickwell, C. J., Pte.

2672 Pidgeon, F. J., Pte.
1765 Pierce, H., Pte.
4270 Pigg, J. T., Pte.
3906 Pinkerton, J. N., Pte.
 736 Pinnock, W. A., Corpl.
1768 Piper, W., Pte.
     Pirie, A. J., Lieut., (M.I.D.)
3882 Pirie, G., Pte.
7537 Pitman, J. T., Pte.
3426 Pitt, E. W., Pte.
3121 Platt, B. M., C.Q.M.S.
2221 Plunkett, A. A., Pte.
4613 Pobjoy, C. J., Pte.
4834 Pogonoski, K. T., Pte.
4570 Pollack, S. J., Pte.
3879 Pollock, C. H., Dvr.
4270 Pollock, G., Sergt.
1981 Polmear, R., Pte.
4271 Polson, O., L/Cpl.
1591 Pont, L., Corpl.
1795 Poole, A. K., Sergt.
7814 Poole, B., Pte.
2676 Pooley, G. P. P., Sergt.
3752 Pooley, R. G., Pte.
2702 Popple, G., Pte.
2671 Porritt, A., T/Cpl., M.M.
2961 Porteous, T., Sergt.
7813 Portors, A., L/Cpl.
3428 Post, J. F., L/Cpl.
3888 Potts, A., Sergt.
     Potts, C. M., Lieut., M.C.
3889 Potts, R., Pte.
3271 Poulson, A., Pte.
4583 Powell, A. W., Pte.
2467 Power, H. M., Pte.
3884 Power, W. E., Pte.
1515 Power, W. J., Pte.
3970 Powers, W. J., Pte.
2525 Pracy, J., Pte.
3190 Prance, T., Corpl.
1980 Presdee, H. C., Pte.
1819 Presland, J. J., Pte.
1978 Prest, A., Pte.
 657 Preston, A., Pte.
2675 Preston, H. H., Pte.
3649 Price, B., Pte.
2424 Price, F. H., Pte.
1979 Price, J., Pte.
5126 Price, J. E., Pte.
3888 Price, W. A., Sergt.
1632 Price, W. S., Pte.
3635 Prime, W. C., Pte.
3988 Prince, H. R., Pte., M.M.
3112 Prince H. V., Pte.
 902 Prince, W. H., Pte.
     Pring, F. P., Lieut.
3426 Pringle, A. E., Corpl.

3640 Pringle, W., Pte.
2669 Proctor, R. L., Sgt.
4878 Proctor, T., Pte.
5438 Proud, A. J., Pte.
6813 Provins, W. D., Pte.
1671 Pryor, D., Pte.
2429 Purcell, D. J., Gun.
7113 Purcell, W. L., Pte.
1757 Purcill, T. M., Pte.
3696 Purser, J. A., Pte.
3613 Pye, A., Pte.
2700 Pye, E. J., Pte.
3437 Pye, J. A., Dvr.
2231 Quartermaine, J. B., Corpl., M.M.
2977 Quaye, J. F., Pte.
4620 Quick, L. A., Pte.
5439 Quick, S. H., Pte.
2954 Quick, W. R., Pte.
3517 Quill, H., Pte.
2225 Quinane, J., Pte.
3440 Quinlan, D. H., Pte.
1826 Quinlan, F., E.R./Cpl.
2706 Quinlan, L. E., Pte.
1815 Quinsey, H. T., Pte.
4226 Rabbitt, A. J., Pte.
1647 Radburn, A., Pte.
2714 Radburn, J., Pte.
2715 Radburn, N., Pte.
7187 Raftery, A. F., Pte.
3706 Ralph, W., Pte.
4278 Ralston, A., Pte.
2981 Ramsay, D. H., Pte.
3888 Ramsay, J. R., Pte.
3906 Ramsey, E., Pte.
1657 Randell, J. C., Pte.
2299 Rankin, J., Pte.
     Rankin, W. E., Lt.
1394 Ranson, W., Pte.
4286 Rattray, G. F., Pte.
4277 Rawson, C. H., L/Cpl. (M.I.D.)
1730 Ray, S. A., Pte.
4621 Ray, F. W. T., Sap.
1982 Rayment, T. G., Pte.
3701 Read, J. R., Pte.
 126 Real, J. J., E.R/2/Cpl., M.M.
 511 Real, P., Pte.
2231 Reddan, B., Pte.
2232 Reddan, J., Pte.
2475 Redpath, G. H., Pte.
15080 Reed, E. B., Pte.
 337 Rees, J., Corpl.
5445 Regan, J., Pte.
     Reid, G. C., Lieut. Hon./Capt., M.C. (M.I.D.)
2495 Reid, J. A., L/Cpl.
3123 Reid, J. A., Pte.
3024 Reid, J. W., Pte.
2982 Reid, P. L., L/Cpl.
2228 Reid, R. A., Pte.
2431 Reid, W. W. B., Pte.

1390 Reidy, T., Pte.
5773 Reilly, C., Pte. (Alias Turner, H.)
3007 Reilly, T., L/Cpl.
1648 Rendell, L. J., Dvr.
2433 Renny, W. L. W., Corpl.
3837 Reoch, R., Pte.
 211 Revie, J., Pte.
4524 Reynolds, B. R., L/Cpl.
3441 Rice, F. H., Pte.
3817 Rice, J., Pte.
6636 Rich, A. J., Pte.
2476 Rich, W. A., Pte.
3709 Richards, A. R., Pte.
3448 Richards, J. G., Pte.
3455 Richards, T., Pte.
2711 Richardson, A. M., A/Sgt.
1984 Richardson, A. V., Pte.
4285 Richardson, C. F. T. Pte.
2516 Richardson, G., Pte.
7118 Richardson, G. T., Pte.
5448 Richardson, J., Pte.
2477 Richardson, W., Pte.
4888 Richter, G. S., Pte.
1986 Ricketts, R. G. W., Pte.
3197 Ridgway, L., Pte.
2712 Ridland, R. J. S., L/Cpl.
     Ridley, J. C. T. E. C. Lt./Col., D.S.O. (M.I.D.)
4286 Rielly, C., Pte.
5156 Riedy, D. H., Pte.
3836 Riley, A. F. A., Pte.
3822 Riley, C. V., Pte.
2230 Riley, F., L/Cpl.
7541 Riley, J. H., Pte.
1759 Riley, T. J., Dvr.
1985 Riley, V., Pte.
1633 Riley, W. G., L/Cpl.
3820 Ring, G. D., Pte.
4622 Risbey, R. J., Pte.
3449 Ritchie, A. F., Corp. M.M.
7820 Ritchie, H. L., Pte.
2175 Roach, M., Pte.
2240 Roach, P., Pte.
4289 Robb, C. G., Pte.
2416 Robbie, N. W. J., Pte.
2555 Robbie, S. D., L/Sgt.
 391 Robbins, P. J., Pte.
3900 Robens, R. J., Pte.
3758 Roberts, A., Pte.
5217 Roberts, E. H., Pte.
1988 Roberts, E. W., Pte. (Stated to be Keith, E. W.)

4902 Searles, E., Corpl.
3119 Secomb, C. L., Corpl.
         M.M.
3406 Seeger, M. A., Corpl.
3225 Seers, G. E. J.,
         L/Cpl.
3459 Seigel, W. W., Pte.
1993 Selems, A. E., Corpl.
2484 Sellick, F. G., Corpl.
         D.C.M.
3393 Seton-Stewart, F. G.,
         Corpl., M.M. and
         Bar.
3450 Seuff, S., Pte.
1634 Sewell, T. F., Pte.
3441 Seymour, D. J., Pte.
2721 Seymour, E. J., Pte.
2504 Shang, C. J., Pte.,
         D.C.M., Bar to
         D.C.M., M.M.
3459 Shanley, F. H. C.,
         Pte., M.M.
3482 Sharp, A. C., Pte.
3440 Sharp, G. J., Pte.
7133 Sharpe, H., Pte.
5459 Sharp, S. E., Pte.
5616 Sharpe, W. H., Pte.
3242 Shaw, A. T., Pte.
1992 Shaw, H. F., Pte.
4428 Shaw, J. E., Pte.
4348 Shearer, G. F.,
         L/Cpl.
2480 Sheather, H., Pte.
1829 Sheffield, P. T., Pte.
3471 Shekell, A., Pte.
2986 Shephard, R. W.,
         Pte.
2731 Shepherd, A. J., Pte.
5107 Sheridan, J., Pte.
1511 Sherrin, R., Pte.
1760 Sherritt, W., Pte.
4528 Sherwin, R. A., Dvr.
1443 Shields, J. C., Pte.
3238 Shipley, G. H., Pte.
5179 Shipp, J. W., Pte.
1994 Shoemark, J. E., Pte.
3148 Shone, J., Corpl.
7832 Short, J., Pte.
4890 Short, J. H., Sapper.
3929 Short, T., Pte.
3460 Shrimpton, R. K.,
         C.S.M.
3983 Shute, A. J., Pte .
4625 Shute, M. G. M.,
         Pte.
1408 Sievwright, J. P., Pte.
3455 Silcocks, C. A., Pte.
1998 Silvester, G., Pte.
2027 Simmons, H. T. Pte.
4242 Simonson, C., L/Cpl.
1456 Simpson, A., Pte.
         Simpson, G. A.,
         Lieut., M.M.
4527 Simpson, G. H., Sgt.
         M.M.

1500 Simpson, H. G.,
         Pte.
3241 Simpson, J., E.R./
         2/Sgt.
2861 Simpson, J. J., Pte.
1997 Simpson, R. A.,
         Corpl. (M.I.D.)
4536 Simpson, W. G., Pte.
4666 Sinclair, E., Pte.
1995 Sinclair, J., Pte.
3920 Sinclair, J., Dvr.
3496 Sindel, R. C., L/Cpl.
1996 Single, F. D., Pte.
4645 Singleton, G., Pte.
3444 Singleton, W., Pte.
         Sinclair, R., Lieut.
2485 Skerritt, A. V., Pte.
1807 Sketheway, T. W.,
         Dvr.
2483 Slavin, P., Pte.
436 Slee, A. T., Pte.
7123 Sloane, J., Pte.
3918 Small, C., Pte.
784 Smart, C., Pte.,
         M.M.
1225 Smiles, P., Pte.
7134 Smiles, R. G., Pte.
1698 Smith, A., Pte.
3233 Smith, A., Pte.
2482 Smith, A. E., Pte.
3458 Smith, A. E., Pte.
2001 Smith, A. H., Pte.,
         M.M.
1999 Smith, B. O., Pte.
1724 Smith, B. R., Sergt.
3446 Smith, C., Pte.
         (Stated to be
         Keats, C. M.)
4477 Smith, C., Sergt.,
         D.C.M.
1834 Smith, C. A., Pte.
3715 Smith, C. C. J., Pte.
         M.M.
4409 Smith, C. G., Pte
514 Smith, C. S., Corpl.
1103 Smith, C. W., Pte.
3207 Smith, E. E., Pte.
1710 Smith, E. F., Sap.
2828 Smith, E. J., Dvr.
3484 Smith, E. P., Pte.
2687 Smith, E. T., Gun.
3015 Smith, F., Pte.
2000 Smith, F. G., Corpl.
2239 Smith, F. R., Pte.
3907 Smith, F. S., Pte.
1690 Smith, F. W., Pte.
3230 Smith, F. W., Pte.
1957 Smith, G. C., Pte.
         Smfth, G. H., Lieut.
2534 Smith, G. J., L/Cpl.
3759 Smith, H., Pte.
4526 Smith, H., Pte.
3240 Smith, H. E., Pte.
7535 Smith, H. E., Pte.
1688 Smith, H. G., Pte.

4531 Smith, H. G., Corpl.
3828 Smith, H. L., Pte.
2703 Smith, J., Pte.
5265 Smith, J. G., Dvr.
3158 Smith, J. J., Sergt.
3475 Smith, J. L., Pte.
2730 Smith, J. W., Pte.
3928 Smith, L., Pte.
2782 Smith, M., Pte.
3714 Smith, N. H., Pte.
2244 Smith, P., Pte.
2238 Smith, R. J., 2/Cpl.
1725 Smith, R. W., Corpl.
1689 Smith, S., Pte.
1837 Smith, S., Pte.
1726 Smith, T. G., Pte.
4900 Smith, W., Pte.
2237 Smith, W. E., L/Cpl.
3463 Smith, W. G., Gun.
3013 Smith, W. H., Pte.
3234 Smith, W. P., Pte.
         Smythe, L. C., Lieut.
1458 Sneesby, C., Pte.
3215 Sneesby, W. R., Pte.
2236 Snook, H. J., Pte.
2682 Solomon, W., Pte.
2445 Somerville, A., Pte.
3026 Somerville, J. T.,
         Pte.
4593 Somerville, R. A.,
         Pte.
3712 Soper, J. S., Pte.
3711 Sorensen, J. F. C.,
         Pte.
         Sorrell, J. H. A.,
         Capt., M.M.
3720 South, C. B., Pte.
2504 South, C., Pte.
2534 Southgate, F. J., Pte.
3021 Sowden, M. C., Pte.
3989 Sowter, C. S., Pte.
3447 Sparkes, R., Pte.
15264 Sparkes, W. E., Pte.
1811 Spedding, J., Pte.
2729 Spence, G. E., Pte.
3124 Spence, P., Sergt.
3508 Spencer, A. B., Pte.
7827 Spencer, T. W., Pte.
3454 Spicer, D. C., L/Cpl.
1614 Spicer, R. W. A.,
         Corpl.
3123 Spicer, W. J., Pte.
2446 Spinks, O. H., Pte.
3443 Spong, C. B., Pte.
7824 Spry, A. E., Pte.
1409 Squires, A. C., Sgt.,
         M.M.
3481 Staddon, W. T.,
         T/Dvr.
14729 Stafford, G. M.,
         Pte.
991 Stafford, W. T.,
         Pte.
4308 Stanley, B., Pte.
2035 Stansfield, J., Pte.
2036 Stansfield, R., Pte.

2489 Thorp, D. E., Pte.
2246 Thorpe, E. J., Pte.
2247 Thorp, F., Pte.
6861 Thorpe, C. W., Pte.
2241 Thow, R., L/Cpl.
3159 Thurecht, N. D., T/Sgt. M.M.
2541 Thurman, W., Pte.
2009 Thurston, H. F., Pte.
2008 Thurston, J., Pte.
444 Tibbenham, S., Sergt.
3127 Tibbey, R. A., Corpl.
4616 Tickner, V. C., Pte.
4254 Tidy, H., Sergt., C. de G. Belgian.
2488 Tilbrook, J., Pte.
2979 Tilbrook, W. C., Corpl.
2917 Tilley, W. A., Pte.
2491 Timothy, E. E., L/Cpl.
Tingcombe, W. N., Lieut.
2012 Tinkler, U., Pte.
2726 Toft. A. S., Pte., M.M.
788 Tolmie, N. A., Sgt.
3246 Tom, C. M., Pte.
2487 Tomlinson, A. E., Pte.
1840 Tomlinson, W., L/Cpl.
2243 Tookey, A. C. W., Pte.
6888 Tookey, W. J., Pte.
3728 Toomey, R. M., Pte.
3461 Toomey, S. T., Pte.
3509 Topham, W. A., Pte.
3248 Topham, W. S., Pte.
2848 Tormey, D., Pte.
1420 Toulson, G., Corpl.
3723 Townrow, C. J., Pte.
2354 Towns, L. L., Pte. (Alias Brand, E.)
2732 Townsend, F., Pte.
2915 Townsend, J. M., Pte.
3286 Tozer, J., Pte.
3253 Tozer, W. C., Corp., M.M.
1672 Tracy, A. J., Pte.
2740 Tracey, F., Pte.
1673 Tracy, R. T., Pte.
1674 Tracy, J., Pte.
1395 Traill, R. C., Sergt.
2733 Travers, W., Pte.
3144 Tregear, A. H., Pte.
3527 Tregear, C. J., Pte.
2048 Trelevan, W., Pte.
3245 Treloar, D., L/Cpl.
3731 Tremain, J. E., Pte.
3937 Trevarthen, A. H., Corpl.
1738 Trevena, C. G., Pte.
1841 Triglone, T. R., Corpl.

3727 Turnbull, M., Pte.,
2371 Troon, B. A., Pte.
8349 Trundle, A. J., Corpl.
2451 Trussell, J., Pte.
3761 Tucker, J. E., Pte.
2989 Tudor, J. R. R., Pte.
3729 Tuite, C., Pte.
2988 Tulley, C. E., Pte.
1967 Tulley, E. H., L/Cpl.
3941 Tunks, S. E. J., Cpl.
3727 Turnbull, M., Pte.
4900 Turner, A., Pte., M.M.
1761 Turner, C. G., Pte.
2738 Turner, F., Pte.
1410 Turner, G., Corpl., M.M.
1334 Turner, J. A., Sgt., (Stated to be Garden, A.)
2737 Turner, J. E., Pte.
4081 Turner, J. J., Pte.
2734 Turner, R. E., Pte.
4047 Turner, S. G., Pte.
2239 Turner, S. T., Pte.
3484 Turner, W. T., E.R./Sgt.
4902 Turvey, T. H., Pte., M.M.
572 Tuson, E. V., W.O., M.C., M.M. (M.I.D.)
2736 Twiss, H. J., Pte.
4618 Twomey, J., Pte.
15265 Twomey, T., Pte.
3408 Tyler, A. H., Pte.
3250 Tyrrell, H. H., Dvr.
2741 Tyrrell, W. A., Pte.
7566 Ulm, C. T. P., Pte.
Upton, E. P. C., Lieut. (M.I.D.)
2742 Vale, W. D., Pte.
3132 Valentine, B., Pte.
3733 Vandyck H., Pte.
1675 Varcoe, C. A. G., Pte.
1951 Varcoe, W. G., Pte.
Varley, A. L., Cant. M.C. and Bar (M.I.D.)
1603 Varney, H. E., L/Cpl.
4659 Varney, W., Sergt.
3762 Vaux, W. R., Pte.
4260 Vaughan, T., L/Cpl.
3949 Veitch, G. C., Pte.
2763 Veitch, R. S., L/Cpl.
3948 Venables, C. H., Corpl., M.M.
1848 Venus, C. A., Pte.
7845 Vernham, C. W., Pte.
3038 Verrall, F. H., Pte., M.M.
1749 Verran, W. J., Pte.

2743 Vidler, W. D., Pte.
Vincent, J., Lieut., M.C. and Bar., D.C.M. (M.I.D.)
2991 Vincin, R. H., Pte.
1748 Vine, E. T., Pte.
3947 Vinnicombe, C. G., Gunner.
1781 Vinicombe, H., Pte.
4615 Vintiner, F. G., Dvr.
2014 Vockler, W. R., Corpl.
3162 Wadds, F. P., L/Cpl.
2499 Wade, G., Pte.
2696 Wade, W. G., L/Cpl., M.M.
4911 Wagner, D. J., Pte.
1758 Wakefield, H. H., Pte., M.M.
4625 Walden, H. T., Pte.
4611 Waldock, A., Sergt.
226 Walford, D. V., Sgt.
2255 Walker, A., Pte.
4537 Walker, A. J., Pte.
Walker, C. N., Lieut.
2993 Walker, E. D., Pte.
2966 Walker, F. C., Sap.
2027 Walker, G. H., Pte.
2193 Walker, J., Sergt., (M.I.D.)
3735 Walker, J. B., L/Cpl.
3744 Walker, L. G., Pte.
2502 Walker, P. O., Pte.
2452 Walker, R. A., Sgt., M.M.
2028 Walker, V. K., L/Cpl.
1661 Walker, W. J., Pte.
2454 Wall, A., Pte.
3518 Wall, A. W., Corpl.
2017 Wall, G., Pte.
2455 Wall, G. W., Pte.
1756 Wallace, De L. J., Sergt.
3972 Wallace, E. J., Sgt. M.M.
2249 Wallace, H. J., Pte.
3736 Wallace, J., Pte., M.M.
3156 Wallace, M., Pte.
3757 Wallace, R. G., Pte., M.M.
7826 Wallace, W. W., E.R./2/Cpl.
1117 Wallen, W .H., Pte.
2994 Wallis, H. E., Pte.
958 Walls, I., Pte.
2497 Walmsley, K., Pte.
3513 Walmsley, R. L., Pte.
2745 Walsh, E., Pte.
2505 Walsh, E., Pte. (Stated to be Crimmins,, E. P. J.)
1853 Walsh, F., Pte.

7334 Williams, C., Pte. (Stated to be Watsford, C. W.)
2507 Williams, C. G., Pte.
2464 Williams, C. J., Pte.
2251 Williams, D., Pte.
1871 Williams, E. G., Pte.
Williams, E. O., Capt., M.C.
2508 Williams, E. S., Pte.
2257 Williams, G. E. G., Dvr.
4322 Williams, G. R., Pte.
2542 Williams, H. G. B., Sergt.
2280 Williams, H. S., Sgt. H/C.S.M.
2208 Williams, J. H., Pte.
3520 Williams, J. J., Pte.
1763 Williams, J. E., Pte.
2273 Williams, P. J., Pte.
1846 Williams, R. H., Sergt.
2210 Williams, R. T. K., Pte.
3287 Williams, S., Pte.
4482 Williams, S., Dvr.
3756 Williams, V. O., Pte.
2496 Williams, W., Pte.
2992 Williams, W., Sergt., D.C.M.
2503 Williamson, G. E. P., Pte.
1713 Williamson, H. N., Pte.
4894 Williamson, J., Pte.
2315 Williamson, J. V., L/Cpl.
5482 Williamson, R., Pte.
2467 Williamson, R. T., Pte.
3958 Williamson, T., Pte.
3747 Williamson, W. J., Pte. (Stated to be Williamson, W.)
3549 Willis., H. P., L/Cpl., M.M.
4915 Willes, J., Pte.
2023 Wills, A. C., Pte.
2022 Wills, C., E.R./Cpl.
3743 Wills, W., Pte.

3140 Wills, W. J., Corpl.
3870 Wilson, A., Pte.
4332 Wilson, A. C., Pte.
1699 Wilson, C. H., Pte., M.M.
4322 Wilson, E. W., Sgt.
2021 Wilson, F., L/Cpl.
2764 Wilson, G. E. V., Pte.
7143 Wilson, G. T., Pte.
4627 Wilson, H., L/Cpl.
2099 Wilson, H. E., Corp.
2250 Wilson, J., Pte.
3515 Wilson, J., Pte.
3734 Wilson, J., Pte.
2020 Wilson, J. W., Pte.
2504 Wilson, N., Pte.
2068 Wilson, R H. L., Pte.
4910 Wilson, R. J., Pte.
2997 Wilson, S., Pte.
2998 Wilson, T., Pte.
3257 Wilson, T. O. P., Pte.
2783 Wilson, W. B., Pte.
4336 Wilson, W. H., L/Cpl.
3225 Winnett, J. M., Pte.
1239 Winney, A. E., Pte.
2734 Winter, G., Pte.
3470 Winter, W. H., Pte.
796 Wise, J. P., C.S.M., M.S.M.
2995 Wiseman, A. J., Sap.
1852 Witney, W. S., Gun.
2740 Witton, G. F., Pte., M.M.
2753 Wolfe, F. W., Pte.
5216 Wolfe, R. E., Pte.
16243 Wolfenden, E. L., Pte.
3961 Wood, A. C. H., Dvr.
2501 Wood, C., Pte.
1764 Wood, F., Pte.
3513 Wood, F. H., Pte.
4338 Wood, H. J., L/Cpl.
4638 Wood, H. V., Pte.
15266 Wood, J., Pte.
2500 Wood, S. R., Pte.
7854 Wood, W. P., Pte.

460 Woodward, F. A., Corpl.
15516 Woodward, F. J., Pte.
14281 Woodward, G., Pte.
7858 Woolage, W. H., Pte.
3511 Woolaston, R. P., Pte.
7857 Wooldridge, P. B., Pte.
2747 Woolf, D., Pte.
3479 Woolfe, F. (Jun.) E.R./Sgt.
2024 Woolbank, S. R., L/Cpl.
2701 Wootton, A. P., Gunner.
2776 Wootton, F. G., Pte.
2025 Wootton, S. K., Pte.
4346 Worner, W. J., Corpl., M.M.
732 Wotton, H. F., Pte.
3138 Wrangham, W., Pte.
7847 Wright, A. E., Pte.
2750 Wright, W., Pte.
3499 Wright, W. E., Pte.
447 Wyatt, H. W., Corp.
3746 Wymer, G. O., Pte.
2510 Yansen, J. A., Pte.
3146 Yeo, T. W., Pte.
3477 Yonker, H., E.R./Sgt.
3476 Young, A. G., Pte.
Young, C. E., Capt., D.S.O. (M.I.D.)
2707 Young, G. L., Gun.
3475 Young, H., Pte.
800 Young, H. E., L/Cpl., M.M.
2030 Young, H. G., Dvr.
4543 Young, H. S., Sap.
Young, J., Lieut., M.C., D.C.M,, (M.I.D.)
2708 Young, P., Pte.
1712 Young, W. G., Pte.
Young, W L., Cap. M.C. (M.I.D.)
579 Zenewich, P., Pte.
2967 Zirbels, F. W., Pte.